Inhaltsverzeichnis

Das Lehrwerk *Retail Milestones* bietet praxisnahes Englisch für alle Handlungssituationen im Einzelhandel.

Retail Milestones ist als Lehr- und Arbeitsheft konzipiert. Für die Schülerinnen und Schüler hat das den Vorteil, dass sie die Lösungen zu den Übungen direkt in ihr Buch schreiben können. Das erleichtert insbesondere die Nachbereitung des Erlernten und die selbstständige Vorbereitung auf Klassenarbeiten.

Retail Milestones bietet eine grundlegende Schulung und Vertiefung der zentralen Kompetenzen und führt die Lernenden dabei zielsicher zum Niveau A2 (Waystage) bzw. Niveau B1 (Threshold), das den KMK-Prüfungen zugrunde liegt. Diese Niveaustufen zeichnen sich dadurch aus, dass die Schülerinnen und Schüler

- häufig gebrauchte Ausdrücke verstehen können, die direkt mit ihrem Arbeitsleben zusammenhängen (z.B. Kunden beraten; Informationen zu Preisen, Produkten und Dienstleistungen geben; Werbemaßnahmen durchführen).
- sich in einfachen, routinemäßigen Situationen verständigen können, in denen es um den direkten Austausch von Informationen geht, die mit ihrer Tätigkeit als Verkäufer/in bzw. Einzelhandelskaufmann/frau zusammenhängen.
- über sich und ihren Beruf sprechen und Dinge beschreiben können, die mit ihrer beruflichen Handlungssituation zu tun haben.

Die als Beispiel im Lehrwerk aufgeführte KMK-Musterprüfung der Niveaustufe II (Europäischer Referenzrahmen B1) reflektiert anschaulich die geforderten Kompetenzbereiche: Rezeption (aus Texten und gesprochenen Mitteilungen Informationen zu entnehmen), Produktion (Erstellen von Schriftstücken), Mediation (Texte vom Deutschen oder der Fremdsprache in die jeweils andere Sprache vermitteln oder übersetzen) und Interaktion (in Rollenspielen Gespräche führen).

Jede Unit umfasst acht Seiten:

Check-in stimmt auf die Unit ein. Der Kasten **Am Ende dieser Unit kann ich ...** macht die Lernziele der Unit bereits zu Beginn für die Schülerinnen und Schüler transparent.

Training stellt die Redemittel, den Wortschatz und die Grammatik bereit, die die Schülerinnen und Schüler brauchen, um die Aufgaben im weiteren Verlauf der Unit zu meistern. Auf fünf Seiten finden sich kommunikative Handlungssituationen, Lesetexte, Aufgaben zum Hörverstehen sowie ein abwechlungsreiches Angebot an Übungen, das die Lernenden systematisch auf den praktischen Einsatz der Fremdsprache im Berufsleben sowie auf Klassenarbeiten und Prüfungen vorbereitet. In den **GRAMMAR SPOT**-Kästen werden die wichtigsten Grammatikstrukturen kurz erläutert (eine ausführliche Grammatik befindet sich im Anhang). Die **HIER UND DORT**-Boxen, die interkulturelle Kompetenz vermitteln, und die **Skills**-Boxen, mit Tipps und Übungen zu ausgewählten Fertigkeiten, runden die einzelnen Units ab.

Check-out bietet am Ende jeder Unit abwechslungsreiche Übungen zum Wiederholen der Schwerpunkte der Unit.

Zu Beginn jeder Unit wird ein Internetlink angegeben über den weiterführende Informationen sowie die Tonaufnahmen zum Lehrwerk als MP3-Dateien online abrufbar sind. Gehen Sie dazu auf www.klett.de und geben Sie den betreffenden Onlinelink im Suchfeld ein.

Autor, Berater und Redaktion wünschen Ihnen viel Spaß und Erfolg bei der Arbeit mit diesem Lehrwerk.

Am Ende dieser Unit kann ich ...	= Zusammenfassung der Lernziele
GRAMMAR SPOT	= Erläuterung der wichtigsten Grammatikstrukturen
HIER UND DORT	= Tipps zur interkulturellen Kompetenz
Tipps	= Sprachtipps und Hinweise auf typische Fehler
Skills	= Training ausgewählter Fertigkeiten
Ich kann jetzt ...	= Selbstevaluation
Online Link 808225-0001	= Online Link mit Internetadressen und Tonaufnahmen zum Lehrwerk
01	= Begleit-CD mit Tracknummer
R/P/I/M	= Kompetenztraining mit Übungen zur Sprach[R]ezeption, Sprach[P]roduktion, [I]nteraktion, [M]ediation (Sprachmittlung)

Meeting colleagues 1

Am Ende dieser Unit kann ich …
→ sagen, was andere verkaufen und wo sie arbeiten.
→ sagen, was ich oft oder gewöhnlich in meinem Job mache.
→ über meine Arbeitsaufgaben Auskunft geben und die Waren, die ich verkaufe, nennen.

Online Link 808225-0001

A Jobs and places of work

[P] **1 Why do you work?**
Write down four reasons why you want to work.

I want to work because I'd like to ______________________________

____

[R/P] **2 Which jobs do they do?**
Find out what the people sell and where they work. Write the correct number in the box next to the photo.

1. Hello, my name's Dennis. I sell computers in a home-entertainment shop.

2. Hi, I I work in a jeans shop. My name's Tina.

3. I'm Samira. Hi. I sell shoes.

4. Hi. I'm Karol. I work in a supermarket.

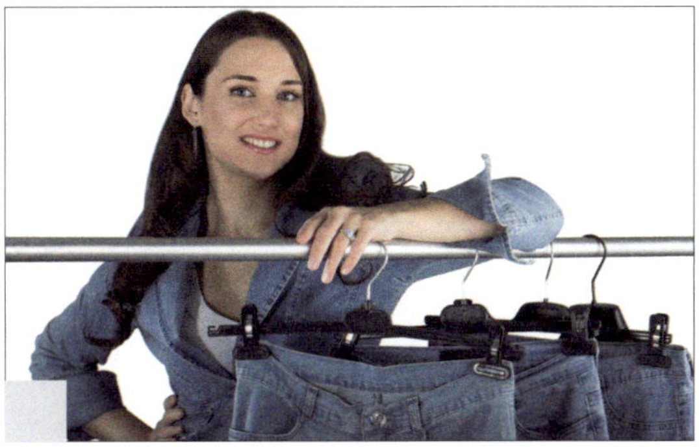

colleague Kollege/Kollegin	**reason** Grund	**home-entertainment shop** Geschäft für Unterhaltungs-elektronik
place of work Arbeitsplatz	**next to** neben	

B Introducing yourself

[R/P] **1 Listening: Visitors from England**

01 Listen to the text and sum it up in one or two sentences.

____

____

[R] **2 Meeting people**

What do the people say when they meet each other? Underline the phrases in the text.

Visitors from England

Fiona, 17, comes from England but she lives in Germany. Together with Anika, 16, she works in a supermarket in Frankfurt which belongs to a big retail chain. They have just started their traineeship after finishing school. Today they are very excited because they are expecting Fiona's friends Steven and Sarah from London. Steven and Sarah are trainees, too, and they work in one of the foreign branches. They are going to visit Fiona for two weeks and they are picking her up from work.

Anika: Look, Fiona. The two at the entrance could be your friends.
Fiona: Yes, they are. I'm so excited, Anika!
Anika: The guy looks nice. Perhaps I can meet him later ...
Fiona: No problem – take your chance! Let's go to them.
Anika: Hi! You must be Steven, right? I'm Anika and well ... you know your friend, Fiona. I'm also a trainee here.
Steven: Hello, you two. Pleased to meet you, Anika. Hi, Fiona. You look as if you need a few days off.
Fiona: You and your funny ideas. I have to work, you know. How are you, Sarah?
Sarah: I'm fine, thanks.
Fiona: Hey, let's go round the shop and get something to drink and eat for tonight.
Anika: Good idea, but we must hurry up because our shop closes at 8 p.m.

Just before they leave the shop, a colleague comes to Fiona.
Frank: Hi, Fiona. Can you tell me where the bottles of wine are? I can't find them and I have to put them on the shelves for tomorrow morning.
Fiona: Oh Frank, they're over there, next to the exit. Let me introduce you to Sarah and Steven. They're friends of mine from England.
Frank: Hi! I'm Frank. Nice to meet you. Sorry, I'm very busy at the moment. See you tomorrow.
Fiona: OK, Frank! Have a nice evening.
Anika: Come on, you three, let's go!

to sum up zusammenfassen
to meet (sich) treffen
to underline unterstreichen
phrase Redewendung
to belong gehören (zu)
retail chain Einzelhandelskette

traineeship Ausbildung
excited aufgeregt
to expect erwarten
trainee Auszubildende/r
foreign branch ausländische Filiale
to pick up abholen

entrance Eingang
Pleased to meet you. Schön Sie/dich/euch kennen zu lernen.
day off freier Tag
shelf Regal

[R] 3 Reading comprehension

Read the text on page 6 and find out if the statements are true or false. Tick (✓) the right box.

	true	false
1. Anika and Fiona are trainees at a supermarket in Germany.	☐	☐
2. Anika, Steven and Sarah are good friends.	☐	☐
3. Frank is a colleague from England.	☐	☐
4. Fiona and her friends want to buy food for the evening.	☐	☐

[I/P] 4 Role play: Introducing yourself

Work in groups of three. Complete the conversation and act it out.

A: Hello. My name's ...

B: Hello. I'm ... May I introduce you to ... (C)?

A: Hi ..., pleased to meet you.

C: Pleased to meet you, too.

A: Are you a trainee, too, ... (B)?

B: Not yet. But I'm hoping to start my traineeship as a(n) ... What do you want to do?

A: I'd like to start as a(n) ...

B: And what are you doing, ... (C)?

C: I'm a trainee ... I work for ...

HIER UND DORT Begrüßung

Bei formellen Begrüßungen verwendet man *"How do you do?"* („Guten Tag."), worauf mit *"How do you do?"* geantwortet wird. Erst dann folgt z.B. die Frage *"How are you?"* („Wie geht es Ihnen/dir?") mit der möglichen Antwort *"I'm fine, thanks."* („Danke, gut.").
Bei gegenseitigem Vorstellen beginnt man formell mit *"May I introduce you to ...?"* („Darf ich Sie ... vorstellen?") oder *"May I introduce ..."* („Darf ich Ihnen ... vorstellen?"), worauf die Antwort folgt *"Pleased/Nice to meet you."* („Ich freue mich, Sie kennen zu lernen."). Unter Freunden begrüßt man sich mit *"Hello."* oder *"Hi."*

[R/M] 5 Vocabulary work

Complete the sentences with the words from the box.

How are you • introduce • meet • retail chain • shelves • traineeship • two days off

1. Pleased to ____________ **(kennen lernen)** you, Mrs Schulz.
2. I think I need ____________ **(zwei Tage frei)**.
3. May I ____________ **(vorstellen)** you to Mr Stein?
4. ____________ **(Wie geht es dir)**, Samira?
5. Many trainees work in shops that belong to a ____________ **(Einzelhandelskette)**.
6. I started my ____________ **(Ausbildung)** a year ago.
7. Every morning I put the goods on the ____________ **(Regale)**.

statement	Aussage	**to introduce sb to sb**	jdn. jdm. vorstellen
to complete	vervollständigen		

C Job duties

branch manager = Filialleiter/in • cashier = Kassierer/in • fashion shop = Modegeschäft • shop assistant = Verkäufer/in

[R/P] **1 Listening: People with different jobs**

02 Listen to three people talking about their jobs. Then fill in the table.

	Torsten Schneider	Ferhat Yilmaz	Jasmin Wesemann
Age			
Town			
Job			
Company			
Duties			

[R/P] **2 Job tasks**

Match the tasks in the box to the photos. Then write a sentence about what each person does. Use the simple present.

serve customers • sort books • tag products • unpack goods

1. Andrej often ______ ______.

2. Anne usually ______ ______.

3. Lin always ______ ______.

4. Orhan rarely ______ ______.

[P] **3 Your job duties**

Write about your own job duties. Use the sentences in exercise 2.

______

______

______

job duty Arbeitsaufgabe	**to match** zuordnen	**to tag** auszeichnen
table Tabelle	**to serve** bedienen	**to unpack** auspacken
company Firma	**customer** Kunde/Kundin	**goods** Waren
task Aufgabe	**to sort** sortieren	

GRAMMAR SPOT Das *simple present*

Denk daran: *he/she/it* – das *s* muss mit!

I	work	get	go
he/she/it	work**s**	get**s**	go**es**
we	work	get	go
you	work	get	go
they	work	get	go

Merke dir die folgenden Häufigkeitsadverbien, die oft in Verbindung mit dem *simple present* verwendet werden: *always* (= immer), *never* (= niemals), *often* (= oft), *rarely* (= selten), *sometimes* (= manchmal), *usually* (= gewöhnlich).

→ Siehe Grammatikanhang auf S. 91.

D Talking about yourself and your job

[R/P] 1 Reading comprehension

Julia's blog

My name's Julia Bachmann and I'm 17 years old. I live in Gifhorn, which is in the north of Germany. At the moment I'm training to become a sales assistant. I work in the fashion department of a big department store in Braunschweig. I start work at 9 o'clock in the morning and I finish at around 8 o'clock in the evening. I'm in the shop only four days a week because I must go to the vocational school once a week. The work is very interesting and I like having contact with customers. But I don't like my boss very much. He's often in a bad mood and I'm afraid to ask him questions. My colleagues at work are really nice. We often help each other and have a lot of fun.

Read Julia's blog. Then tick (✓) the correct answers.

1. Julia Bachmann is
   ☐ a) 10 years old. ☐ b) 17 years old. ☐ c) 18 years old. ☐ d) 25 years old.
2. She starts work at
   ☐ a) 7 o'clock in the morning. ☐ b) 9 a.m. ☐ c) 11 o'clock in the morning. ☐ d) 1 p.m.
3. Why doesn't she like her boss?
   ☐ a) He's too old. ☐ c) He's often in a bad mood.
   ☐ b) He doesn't look nice. ☐ d) He's always in a bad mood.
4. What does Julia like about her job? She likes
   ☐ a) unpacking goods. ☐ b) her teachers. ☐ c) her colleagues. ☐ d) tagging products.

HIER UND DORT Berufsbezeichnungen

Das deutsche System der dualen Ausbildung hat keine direkte Entsprechung in Großbritannien und den USA. Aus diesem Grund können viele deutsche Berufsbezeichnungen nicht einfach übersetzt werden, sondern müssen umschrieben werden.
Zudem gibt es für einige Berufsbezeichnungen in Großbritannien und den USA unterschiedliche Begriffe. So heißt der Verkäufer in Großbritannien z.B. *shop assistant*, während er in den USA oft als *sales assistant*, *sales clerk* oder *salesperson* bezeichnet wird. Beim Einzelhandelskaufmann ist es ähnlich – in Großbritannien nennt man ihn *retailer* oder *shopkeeper*, in den USA ebenfalls *retailer* sowie *retail salesman* oder *storekeeper*.

training to become in der Ausbildung sein zum/zur
department Abteilung
department store Kaufhaus
vocational school Berufsschule
once einmal
to have contact with Kontakt haben mit
mood Stimmung
to be afraid Angst haben

[P] 2 Your own blog
Write a blog about yourself and your job.
Start like this: My name is Toni and I work in ...

→ See phrases on page 12.

[R/P] 3 Products in a supermarket
Write the English names of these products under the photos. Use the words in the box.

bread • chocolate • fruit • magazines

1. ____________ 2. ____________ 3. ____________ 4. ____________

[P/M] 4 Goods at your place of work
Write down some goods that you sell at your place of work. Use a dictionary, if necessary.

____

[I/P] 5 Talking about jobs
Ask a partner where he/she works and what he/she sells. Take notes about your partner's job.

→ See phrases on page 12.

GRAMMAR SPOT Fragebildung im *simple present*
Fragen stellt man mit *do* oder (bei *he*, *she* und *it*) mit *does*.
Beispiel: Where **do** you work and what **do** you sell?
ABER: Where **does** he work and what **does** he sell?

→ Siehe Grammatikanhang auf S. 91.

Skills: Practical dictionary work
You can look up words in a dictionary or on the internet. But be careful:
Many words have more than one meaning.

1 Using a dictionary
Write down the correct German translation for the marked words.

1. I hope that I can **pass** the test next month. ____________
2. Some customers like **jewellery**. ____________
3. This shop has a good **reputation**. ____________
4. My sister wants to **try on** new shoes. ____________

2 Using the internet
Put 'online+Wörterbuch' into a search engine. Look up the words and write down the English translation.

1. Internetzugang = ____________
2. Stichwort = ____________
3. Spielzeugwarengeschäft = ____________
4. Drogerie = ____________

to take notes Notizen machen
meaning Bedeutung
search engine Suchmaschine

E Checking

[R/P] 1 Retail crossword

Fill in the right words.

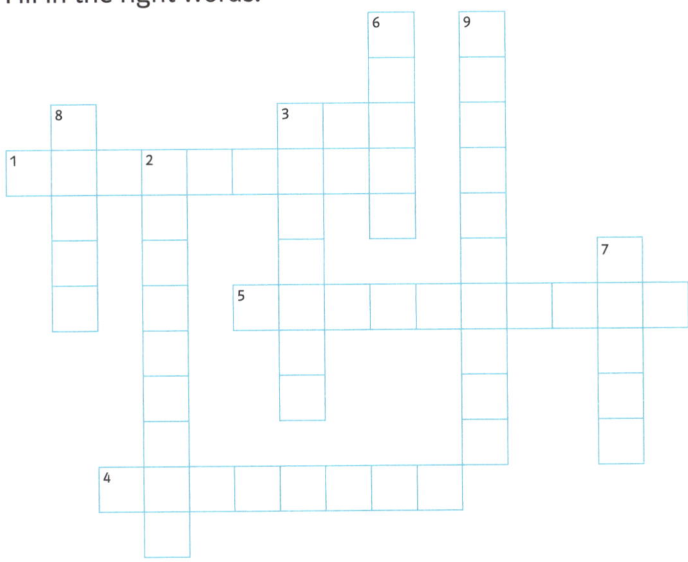

Across:
1. It is sweet and you can eat it.
4. A person who wants to buy something in a shop.
5. You use this book if you want to look up the meaning of a word.

Down:
2. Somebody who works with you at your place of work.
3. You give this person the money when you buy goods in a shop.
6. You pay with it.
7. Another word for apples, bananas, oranges, ...
8. You can put goods on it.
9. A school where you learn more about your job is a ... school.

[R/P] 2 Odd one out

Underline the odd word out in each group. Say why it is different from the other words.
Example: In group 1 ... is the odd one out because ...

1. colleague – trainee – retail chain – branch manager
2. money – buy – shelf – traineeship
3. shop – supermarket – department store – school
4. England – London – Germany – Turkey

[P] 3 Words with the same meaning

Find synonyms for these words. (Tip: All of the words are in Unit 1.)
Example: shop assistant (BE) = sales clerk (AE), salesperson (AE), sales assistant (AE)

1. goods = ____________________
2. hello = ____________________
3. nice to meet you = ____________________
4. retailer = ____________________
5. duty = ____________________

Ich kann jetzt ...

1. mich und andere Personen vorstellen. ○○○
2. sagen, was andere verkaufen und wo sie arbeiten. ○○○
3. sagen, was ich in meinem Job mache. ○○○
4. über meine Arbeitsaufgaben und die Waren, die ich verkaufe Auskunft geben. ○○○
5. mithilfe eines Wörterbuchs und des Internets Wörter richtig übersetzen. ○○○

☺☺☺ = Kann ich schon!
☺☺ = Kann ich ein bisschen!
☺ = Kann ich bald!

odd one out nicht dazugehören

Phrases: Introducing yourself and others

Meeting each other

I'm Peter./My name is Peter Rex.	Ich heiße Peter./Mein Name ist Peter Rex.
Please call me Tina.	Nennen Sie mich doch Tina.
My surname is Krey, my first name is Silke.	Mein Familienname ist Krey, mein Vorname ist Silke.
How do you do?	Guten Tag.
How are you?/How are you doing?	Wie geht es Ihnen/dir? *(informelle Begrüßung)*
I'm fine, thanks.	Danke, gut.
I'm from Berlin, and I'm 20 years old.	Ich stamme aus Berlin und bin 20 Jahre alt.
I'm British/German.	Ich bin Brite/Britin/Deutsche/r.
May I introduce you to Mrs Rogers?	Darf ich Sie Frau Rogers vorstellen?
May I introduce Mr Stein (to you)?	Darf ich Ihnen Herrn Stein vorstellen?
Pleased/Nice to meet you.	Ich freue mich/Schön Sie kennen zu lernen.
And how are you?	Und (wie geht es) Ihnen/dir?

Talking about your training and your work

I'm a trainee shop/sales assistant.	Ich mache eine Ausbildung zum Verkäufer/zur Verkäuferin.
I'm training to become a retailer/shop-keeper/retail salesman/storekeeper.	Ich mache eine Ausbildung zum Einzelhandels-kaufmann/zur Einzelhandelskauffrau.
I started my traineeship in August.	Ich begann meine Ausbildung im August.
I sell many different goods.	Ich verkaufe viele verschiedene Waren.
I sell fruit/shoes/clothing/household goods/toys/textiles/furniture/stationary/sporting goods/electrical appliances.	Ich verkaufe Obst/Schuhe/Kleidung/Haushaltswaren/Spielwaren/Textilien/Möbel/Schreibwaren/Sportartikel/Elektroartikel.
I unpack articles and sort them.	Ich packe Artikel aus und sortiere sie.
I must fill up the shelves tomorrow.	Ich muss morgen die Regale auffüllen.
I often tag the products that we sell.	Ich zeichne oft die Produkte aus, die wir verkaufen.
I sometimes serve customers.	Ich bediene manchmal Kunden.

Products and services 2

Am Ende dieser Unit kann ich ...
- → Produkte und ihre Vorteile beschreiben.
- → Kunden erfolgreich bedienen.
- → Redewendungen im Umgang mit Kunden richtig benutzen.

Online Link 808225-0002

A Describing products

[R/P] **1 Different products**
Use adjectives from the box and write a sentence about each product.

comfortable • delicious • fashionable • healthy • old-fashioned • portable • stylish • well-designed

1. ____________________

3. ____________________

2. ____________________

4. ____________________

[R] **2 Listening: Going shopping**
03 Listen to the text. Then tick (✓) the correct answer.

1. Steven wants to look for
   ☐ a) shoes as well. ☐ b) a new bike. ☐ c) computer parts.
2. Sarah and Fiona go to
   ☐ a) a shoe shop. ☐ b) a supermarket. ☐ c) a department store.
3. Sarah finds a pair of shoes that
   ☐ a) don't fit. ☐ b) are uncomfortable. ☐ c) are stylish.

service	Dienstleistung	**fashionable**	modisch	**portable**	tragbar
comfortable	bequem	**healthy**	gesund	**stylish**	elegant, stilvoll
delicious	köstlich	**old-fashioned**	altmodisch	**well-designed**	gut gestaltet

B Explaining the benefits of products

[R/P] 1 Reading comprehension

Going shopping

It is 9 o'clock in the morning. Fiona, Steven and Sarah are having breakfast. They have just decided to go on a shopping tour. About half an hour later they are in the city centre.

Sarah: Let's go to a shoe shop first.
Steven: Oh, dear! You and your shoes! I'd like to go to a department store and look for an external hard drive. OK? I'm coming home in the afternoon.
Fiona: All right, Steven. Good luck! Hey, Sarah, perhaps they're having some special offers in the shoe shop over there.
Sarah: Yes, maybe. But you know: good quality has its price.
Fiona: Come on, Sarah. This shop looks attractive. Let's see what they have.

Fiona and Sarah enter the shop and Sarah soon finds a pair of shoes that she likes.

Sarah: This pair of shoes is great, isn't it?
Fiona: Yes, but they're quite expensive.
Sarah: So, what? I'm going to try them on, Fiona. It's a must! ... Well, what do you think of them?
Fiona: They look great, Sarah! Do they fit?
Sarah: Yes, they do and they go well with my trousers.
Fiona: They suit you and your stylish clothing.
Sarah: I hope I can attract some nice boys with my new shoes at the disco next time.
Fiona: Let's see. Come on, Sarah! I still want to buy some clothes.
Sarah: Don't worry, Fiona! As you know there are lots of good fashion shops here.

Read the text and answer the questions in complete sentences.

1. When do Fiona, Steven and Sarah decide to go shopping?

____

2. What does Sarah say about the price and quality of products?

____

3. Who does Sarah want to attract with her new shoes at the disco?

____

4. What does Fiona want to buy?

____

benefit	Nutzen	**special offer**	Sonderangebot	**to fit**	passen
to decide	entscheiden	**attractive**	attraktiv	**to go well with**	gut passen zu
external hard drive	externe Festplatte	**to enter**	betreten	**to suit**	(jdm.) stehen

[P/I] **2 Which product is it?**
Make a list of five products and show it to a partner. Then describe a product from your list. Your partner tries to guess which one it is. Then change roles.
Example: It's small and you can store things from your computer on it. (= USB stick)

[P] **3 What are the people doing?**
Write down what the people are doing. Use the present continuous.

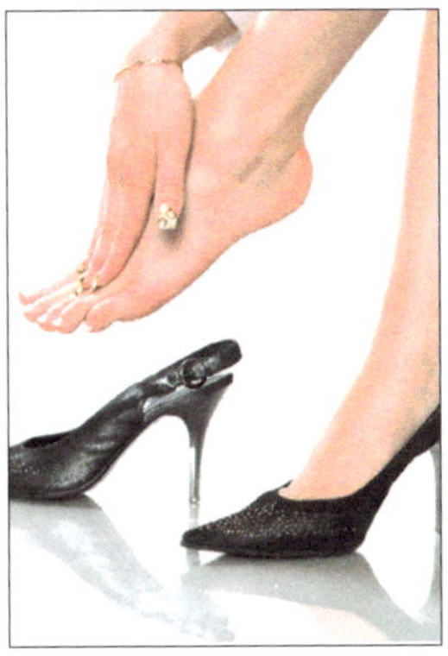

1. ______________
2. ______________
3. ______________
4. ______________

GRAMMAR SPOT Das *present continuous*

Aussage	Verneinung	Frage
I am (I'm) helping	I'm not helping	Am I helping?
you are (you're) working	you aren't working	Are you still working here?
he/she/it is (he's/she's/it's) looking	he/she/it isn't looking	Isn't he/she/it looking fantastic?
we are (we're) going	we aren't going	Are we going home now?
you are (you're) working	you aren't working	Are you still working?
they are (they're) unpacking	they aren't unpacking	Are they still unpacking books?

→ Siehe Grammatikanhang auf S. 92.

Das *present continuous* wird verwendet für
1. Handlungen, die im Moment stattfinden.
   Beispiel: *He **is unpacking** shoes now. They **are starting** their traineeship today.*
2. Handlungen, die auf einen (gegenwärtigen) Zeitraum begrenzt bzw. nicht abgeschlossen sind.
   Beispiel: *She **is living** in England this year. We **are staying** in Braunschweig this week.*
3. zukünftige Handlungen (mit Zeitbestimmung).
   Beispiel: *I **am serving** customers this afternoon. They **are closing** at one o'clock.*

Typische Zeitangaben, in Verbindung mit dem *present continuous*, sind: *at the moment* (= im Augenblick), *just* (= gerade), *now* (= jetzt), *still* (= noch immer).

to describe beschreiben
to guess (er)raten
to change tauschen, wechseln
to store (ab)speichern

[P/I] 4 At the fashion shop

Write down what Fiona and Sarah are saying. Then practise the dialogue with a partner.
Example: *Sarah:* (What/you/look/for), Fiona? → What are you looking for, Fiona?

1. *Fiona:* **(I/search for/a fashionable blouse)**

   ____

2. *Sarah:* **(you/look for/a colourful blouse?)**

   ____

3. *Fiona:* No, **(I/think of/something/simple)**, Sarah. Like this one.

   ____

4. *Sarah:* Fine. I'll look around **(while/you/try it on)**

   ____

5. *Fiona:* **(I/take/this/one)** I love it!

   ____

C Talking to customers

[R/P] 1 Reading comprehension

In the department store

Steven has just entered the computer department when he meets Peter, a young shop assistant.

Steven: Excuse me, Sir. Do you speak English?
Peter: Good morning, Sir. Yes, I do. Are you being served?
Steven: Not yet. I'm looking for an external hard drive. They seem to be cheaper here than in Britain.
Peter: I don't know the prices in Britain but we've got some hard drives on offer, right over there. Which ones are you particularly interested in?
Steven: I'm looking for one which is portable and runs on my computer system.
Peter: No problem, Sir. Have a look at this product. It's a special offer and it has a storage capacity of 500 GB.
Steven: Well, I'm actually looking for something smaller.
Peter: Let me show you this one then. It's smaller and has a storage capacity of 120 GB.
Steven: That's fine. I've heard that small hard drives are faster than bigger ones. Is that true?
Peter: It's partly true, Sir. Have a look at this one. It's small and it offers you the same storage capacity as the large one but it's faster.
Steven: And the price tag tells me that there's hardly any difference in price compared with the other hard drives.
Peter: That's right, Sir. I think it's a very good bargain.
Steven: I think so, too. Thank you for your help.
Peter: You're welcome. The cash desk is right over there.

to practise üben
particularly besonders
storage capacity Speicherkapazität
actually eigentlich
partly teilweise
to offer (an)bieten
price tag Preisschild
hardly kaum
to compare (with/to) vergleichen (mit
bargain Schnäppchen
You're welcome. Bitte schön, gern geschehen.
cash desk Kasse

Read the text on page 16. Then complete the sentences with words from the text.

Steven wants to buy an (1) ______________________. The products are (2) ______________ than in Britain. The (3) ______________________ shows him some hard drives that they have (4) ______________. Steven thinks the one with a (5) ________________ of 120 GB is OK. He likes it because it is (6) ______________, very fast and runs on his (7) ____________________. He thinks it is a good (8)__________ and he buys it.

[P/I] **2 Role play: Sales talk**

Work with a partner. Partner A is a customer who wants to buy a product (for example, a television/a car/...). Partner B is a shop assistant. Use the dialogue on page 16 and change it where necessary. Practise the dialogue and then act it out in class.

→ See phrases on page 20.

HIER UND DORT Kunden bedienen

Es ist wichtig, Kunden freundlich und höflich anzusprechen. Manche englischen Redewendungen klingen für Deutsche übertrieben höflich oder werden im Deutschen nicht verwendet. Dennoch sollten Sie diese beherrschen.

1. **Begrüßung**
   "Good morning/afternoon/evening, Sir/Madam./Excuse me, Sir/Madam. Can I help you?/ Is there anything I can do for you?/Are you being served, Sir/Madam?/How can I help you?"
2. **Redewendungen im Laufe des Kundengesprächs**
   "Are you interested in ...?/Would you like to ...?/Have a look at .../Let me show you .../What about ...?/Anything else, Sir/Madam?"
3. **Verabschiedung des Kunden**
   a) nach einem Verkaufsgespräch: Im Allgemeinen verabschiedet sich der Kunde/die Kundin mit *"Thank you for your help."* Darauf sollten Sie mit *"You're welcome."* antworten. Sollte der Kunde/die Kundin nichts sagen, können Sie mit *"We hope to see you again soon, Sir/Madam."* das Gespräch beenden.
   b) an der Kasse nach dem Bezahlen: *"Here you are, Sir/Madam. Your change and your receipt. Thank you very much for shopping with us. Have a nice day."*

D Serving customers successfully

[R/P] **1 Listening: Serving customers**

04

Listen to the three conversations. Then match the dialogues 1–3 to the photos A–C.

A

B

C

______________ ______________ ______________

successfully erfolgreich	**drill** Bohrmaschine	**receipt** Quittung, Kassenzettel
sausage Würstchen	**acceptable** akzeptabel	
certainly sicherlich	**change** Wechselgeld	

[R/P] 2 **Talking to customers**
04 Use the words in the box and fill in the missing phrases. Listen again and check your answers.

Dialogue 1

Assistant: (1) ____________ How can I help you?
Customer: I'd like to buy some sausages.
Assistant: Certainly, Sir. (2) ____________
Customer: Five, please.
Assistant: (3) ____________
Customer: No, thank you, that's all. Where do I have to pay?
Assistant: (4) ____________

Dialogue 2

Customer: Hello, Sir. (5) ____________
Assistant: Yes, of course, Sir. (6) ____________
Customer: I'm looking for a new drill.
Assistant: OK, Sir. (7) ____________
Customer: It looks fine and the price seems acceptable, too.
Assistant: You're right, Sir. (8) ____________
Customer: I'll take it then.
Assistant: Here you are. (9) ____________

Dialogue 3

Assistant: Good evening, Madam. (10) ____________
Customer: (11) ____________ a chicken sandwich and a coke, please.
Assistant: That's 9 euros, please.
Customer: (12) ____________
Assistant: Thanks a lot. (13) ____________

Anything else, Sir? • At the cash desk over there, Sir. • Can you help me, please? • I'd like to have ... • Good morning, Sir. • Here's your change and your receipt. • Here you are. • How many would you like? • It's a real bargain. • Thank you for shopping with us. • What about this one? • What are you looking for? • What can I do for you?

Skills: Vocabulary work
Even if you don't know a word, you can often find out its meaning because you already know a part of the word.
Examples: responsible → **ir**responsible (= *unverantwortlich*), interesting → **un**interesting (= *uninteressant*), to like → to **dis**like (= *nicht mögen*)

1 Prefixes
Guess the meanings of the words without using a dictionary.

1. unhappy = ____________
2. unattractive = ____________
3. incorrect = ____________
4. uncomfortable = ____________
5. non-smoker = ____________
6. disorganised = ____________

2 Checking
Now check your answers with the help of a dictionary.

to miss fehlen, vermissen

E Checking

[M] **1 Say it in English**
Put the sentences into English.

1. Werden Sie schon bedient?
____
2. Wonach suchen Sie?
____
3. Wie wäre es mit diesem Produkt?
____
4. Ich wünsche Ihnen einen schönen Tag.
____

[R/P] **2 Talking to customers**
Match the phrases 1.–5. with the correct answers a)–e). Draw lines.

1. Here you are.
2. Good morning, Sir.
3. Could you help me, please?
4. What product are you interested in?
5. Thank you for your help.

a) You're welcome.
b) Yes, of course.
c) A nice blouse for the summer.
d) Hello.
e) Thank you.

[R/P] **3 Writing a postcard**
Use the verbs in the box and complete the sentences in the present continuous.

drink • eat • enjoy • go (2x) • have (2x) • sing • sit • take • visit • write

Dear David,

How are you? I (1) _______________ you from my trip to Dresden. I (2) _______________ a wonderful time here. At the moment I (3) _______________ breakfast with my cousin Fatima. We (4) _______________ bread with honey and we (5) _______________ tea. The weather is fantastic, so we (6) _______________ in the garden. The birds (7) _______________ and we (8) _______________ ourselves. Soon we (9) _______________ to town. In the afternoon my grandmother (10) _______________ us. At the moment my uncle (11) _______________ her to the doctor. And in the evening we (12) _______________ to the cinema.

Hope to hear from you soon.

Love, Ayşe

Ich kann jetzt ...

1. Produkte und ihre Vorteile beschreiben. ○○○
2. Kunden begrüßen und ihnen Hilfe anbieten. ○○○
3. den Kunden bei der Auswahl von Produkten helfen. ○○○
4. die Kunden nach einem Verkaufsgespräch und an der Kasse richtig verabschieden. ○○○

☺☺☺ = Kann ich schon!
☺☺ = Kann ich ein bisschen!
☺ = Kann ich bald!

to draw zeichnen **to enjoy** genießen **cinema** Kino

Phrases: Serving customers

To greet customers

Hello.	Hallo.
Good morning/afternoon/evening, Sir/Madam.	Guten Morgen/Tag/Abend.
Nice to see you (again), Sir/Madam.	Schön Sie (wieder) zu sehen.

To offer help

Excuse me, Sir/Madam.	Entschuldigen Sie.
Are you being served, Sir/Madam?	Werden Sie schon bedient?
Can I help you?	Kann ich Ihnen helfen?
What can I do for you?	Was kann ich für Sie tun?
How can I help you?	Wie kann ich Ihnen helfen?
Is there anything I can do for you?	Kann ich Ihnen behilflich sein?
Would you like to look around first, Sir/Madam?	Möchten Sie sich erst selbst umsehen?
Let me know if you need any help.	Lassen Sie (es) mich wissen, wenn Sie Hilfe benötigen.

To help customers find a product

What exactly are you looking for?	Wonach suchen Sie genau?
What do you need the product for?	Wofür brauchen Sie das Produkt?
What about this product?	Wie wäre es mit diesem Produkt?
Have a (closer) look at this product.	Sehen Sie sich dieses Produkt mal (genauer) an.
Let me show you how it works.	Lassen Sie mich Ihnen zeigen wie es funktioniert.
How much money do you want to spend on the product?	Wieviel Geld möchten Sie für das Produkt ausgeben?

To show the benefits of a product

The product is comfortable/delicious/fashionable/healthy/old-fashioned/reliable/portable/stylish/well-designed.	Das Produkt ist bequem/köstlich/modisch/gesund/altmodisch/zuverlässig/tragbar/stilvoll/gut gestaltet.
The product helps you to (+ *infinitive*) ...	Das Produkt hilft Ihnen ...
It allows you to/enables you to ...	Es erlaubt/gestattet Ihnen ...
It is made of ...	Es ist hergestellt aus ...
It was made in ...	Es wurde in ... hergestellt.
It is/can be used for (+ *-ing-form*) ...	Es wird/kann verwendet werden für ...

To close a sales talk

Is there anything else I can do for you?	Gibt es noch etwas, das ich für Sie tun kann?
You're welcome.	Bitte schön, gern geschehen.
We hope to see you again soon, Sir/Madam.	Wir hoffen Sie bald wieder zu sehen.
Here you are, Sir/Madam. Your change and your receipt.	Hier bitte schön. Ihr Wechselgeld und Ihre Quittung.
Thank you for shopping with us.	Vielen Dank für Ihren Einkauf.
Have a nice day.	Ich wünsche Ihnen noch einen schönen Tag.

Customers 3

Am Ende dieser Unit kann ich ...

→ verschiedene Kundentypen unterscheiden und deren Einkaufsgewohnheiten benennen.
→ mich auf verschiedene Kundengruppen einstellen.
→ typische Merkmale verschiedener Geschäfte nennen.

Online Link 808225-0003

A Types of customers and their shopping habits

[R/P] 05 **1 Listening: Different types of customers**
Listen to the description of different types of customers. Then look at the photos and write down what type of customer they show. Use the words in the box.

1. ______________________

3. ______________________

customers of habit • green customer • hectic customer • sceptic customer

2. ______________________

4. ______________________

[P] **2 Identify yourself**
What type of customer are you? Write two sentences about yourself.
Start like this: I'm a ... customer because ...

____

____

[P/I] **3 Talk to each other**
Ask a partner what type of customer he/she is. Then present him/her in class.
Start like this: Daniel is a green customer because ...

habit Gewohnheit
sceptic skeptisch, kritisch
behaviour Verhalten
to distinguish unterscheiden
environmentally friendly umweltfreundlich
to leave (ver)lassen
packaging Verpackung
carefully sorgfältig
to identify identifizieren
to take one's time sich Zeit nehmen
in a hurry in Eile

B Keeping customers satisfied

[R/P] **1 Adapting to different customers**

Decide how you would react in the following situations and tick (✓) the right box. Then read the box below and check your answers.

1. A customer always looks at his watch and runs through the shop. He takes the things he needs and puts them into his trolley. He seems to know what he wants.
   I should ☐ a) do nothing.
   ☐ b) ask, "Can I help you, Sir/Madam?"
   ☐ c) say, "Nice to see you, Sir/Madam."

2. A customer looks at some products and studies the labels. She obviously doesn't know which product she wants to buy.
   I should ☐ a) do nothing.
   ☐ b) greet the customer and ask, "Is there anything I can do for you, Madam?"
   ☐ c) just greet the customer.

3. A customer looks at products made of natural materials. She seems to be comparing different clothes.
   I should ☐ a) greet her and ask, "Are you interested in more information about the products?" Then I should tell her what the products are made of.
   ☐ b) say, "Let me know if you need any help."
   ☐ c) do nothing.

HIER UND DORT Kundentypen und -gruppen

1. **Kundentypen**
   Im Alltag müssen wir uns auf unterschiedliches Kundenverhalten einstellen, um im Verkauf erfolgreich zu sein. Einen Eindruck, ob und wie wir Kunden ansprechen sollten, gewinnen wir durch Beobachtung. Ein Kunde, der sich Hilfe suchend umsieht, möchte wahrscheinlich angesprochen werden. Dagegen eine Kundin, die weiß was sie will und schnell die Waren in den Einkaufswagen packt, würde eine Ansprache eher als störend empfinden.
2. **Kundengruppen: Ausländer, Kinder und Senioren**
   a) Ausländische Kunden sprechen zum Teil kein oder wenig Deutsch und suchen evtl. Produkte, die sie aus ihrer Heimat kennen. Wichtig ist, Verständnis zu zeigen, langsam und in kurzen Sätzen zu sprechen und ggf. das Verwenden der Ware zu demonstrieren.
   b) Kindern sollte ein positives Einkaufserlebnis vermittelt werden. Wir sollten sie grüßen und uns Zeit für sie nehmen. Oftmals hilft es sie anzusprechen (z.B. „Während deine Eltern einkaufen, kannst du ja die Rutsche benutzen."). Sollte das Kind alleine einkaufen, können wir es, je nach Alter, für seine Selbstständigkeit loben.
   c) Senioren sind eine Kundengruppe, die zahlenmäßig zunimmt. Sie verfügen oftmals über ein gesichertes Einkommen und erhebliche Sparbeträge. Sich mit ihnen zu unterhalten erfordert Einfühlungsvermögen und Geduld. Teilweise ist ihr Sehvermögen oder ihre Hörfähigkeit eingeschränkt. Zum Verzehr sollten eher kleinere Packungsgrößen empfohlen werden.

to keep sb satisfied jdn. zufrieden stellen
to adapt (sich) anpassen
to follow folgen
trolley Einkaufswagen
to study studieren, sorgfältig lesen
label Etikett
obviously offensichtlich

[R/P/I] **2 Listening: Helping different groups of customers**

06 Read and listen to the dialogues between different customers and shop assistants. Then choose one dialogue and practise it with a partner.

→ See phrases on page 28.

Dialogue 1

A foreign customer has just entered a DIY-store in Dresden.

Assistant: Guten Tag, wie kann ich Ihnen behilflich sein?
Customer: Good morning, Sir. I'm afraid my German is not good. I'm from Dubai. Do you speak English?
Assistant: No problem, Sir. Please tell me how I can help you.
Customer: I'm looking for a new pump for our swimming pool.
Assistant: OK, Sir. Come with me, please. I'll show you some.
Customer: That's very kind of you. Thank you.
Assistant: Do you need a pump for a small or a big pool?
Customer: Sorry, I don't understand.
Assistant: Please show me how big your swimming pool is.
Customer: It's this size, Sir.
Assistant: Then this is the right pump for you. It also comes with a guarantee.
Customer: Thank you very much. I'll buy it.
Assistant: You're welcome, Sir. Have a nice day.

Dialogue 2

A family is looking for a picture frame in a big photographic shop. The kids are getting on their parents' nerves. The shop assistant hears them talking in English.

Assistant: Sorry to disturb you. Can I help you?
Man: Thank you, but we don't need any help.
Assistant: All right. I'd like to tell you that we have a special kids' zone. We take care of your children there while you're doing your shopping.
Man: Well, that's interesting. Where is it?
Assistant: It's near the entrance, Sir. If you wish, I can take your children there. You can pick them up when you've finished your shopping.
Woman: That's great. Let's do that. Then we'll have time for our shopping.

Dialogue 3

An elderly couple is comparing prices of different packages of butter. They are tourists from an English-speaking country.

Assistant: Good morning. Do you need any help?
Woman: Yes, I'm afraid we do. We can't really read the prices. They're so small.
Assistant: No problem, Madam. I can read them out to you. This package costs 1 euro and this one is 2 euros. Is there anything else I can do for you?
Man: Pardon?
Assistant: Is there anything else I can do for you?
Man: No, thank you. You were very helpful.

to choose	wählen	**guarantee**	Garantie	**kids' zone**	Kinderbereich
DIY-store	Baumarkt	**picture frame**	Bilderrahmen	**to take care of**	aufpassen auf
pump	Pumpe	**to get on sb's nerves**	jdm. auf die Nerven gehen	**elderly**	älter
kind	freundlich	**to disturb**	stören	**couple**	Paar
size	Größe				

C Different types of shops

[R/P] ◎ 07

1 Listening: Types of shops

Look at the photos and describe what you see. Then listen to the text and put the pictures in the right order. Write the correct number in the box next to the photo.

[R/P] ◎ 07

2 Advantages of different shops

Listen again. Then put the words in the correct order and add the name of the right type of shop.

Example: a/where/near/live/is/people/? → A corner shop is near where people live.

1. at/people/old/often/products/buy/a/?

   ____

2. can/cheap/you/buy/at/food/a/?

   ____

3. designs/has/a/in/products/different/?

   ____

4. are/help/you/there/assistants/at/shop/can/who/you/?

   ____

[P/I]

3 Which shops do you like?

Ask three people in your class about the type of shop they like best and why they go there. Take notes and present your results in class.

specialist shop Fachgeschäft	**to collect** (ein)sammeln	**to count** zählen
corner shop (kleines) Lebensmittelgeschäft	**discounter** Billigsupermarkt	**design** Gestaltung
far away weit weg	**to earn** verdienen	**advantage** Vorteil
owner Besitzer/in	**shop fittings** Ladenausstattung	**to add** hinzufügen
		result Ergebnis

D Future plans

[R] 1 Your life in ten years

You are taking part in a survey called: "How do you see your life in ten years?"
Read the questions and tick (✓) the right answer.

Questions	Yes, I will.	No, I won't.	I don't know.
1. I will have lots of money.			
2. I will have a good job.			
3. I will live in another country.			
4. I will have a nice car.			
5. I will own a house.			
6. I will be married.			

[P/I] 2 Talking about the future

Work in groups. Say how you see your life in ten years and why.
Start like this: I think I will .../I don't think I will .../I don't know ...

[P/I] 3 Plans for the weekend

Talk to a partner about his/her plans for the next weekend.
Example: *Partner A:* What are you going to do on Friday?
Partner B: I think I'm going to go to the cinema.

[R] 4 Future tenses

Underline the correct answer.

1. I hope that he **will/is going to** visit us tomorrow.
2. We **will/are going to** meet at school every Monday.
3. They think she **will/is going to** buy a new car.
4. I know you **will/are going to** be on holiday next month.

GRAMMAR SPOT Das Futur

Will-future

Will und *won't* bleiben in allen Personen unverändert.

→ Siehe Grammatikanhang auf S. 95.

I will ('ll) visit	I won't visit
he/she/it will ('ll) visit	he/she/it won't visit
we/you/they will ('ll) visit	we/you/they won't visit

Das *will-future* wird verwendet, um Tatsachen, Vorhersagen und Vermutungen zu äußern.
Beispiel: *In 2020 I'**ll be** 30 years old. I think I'**ll have** a good job then.*

Going to-future

Diese Zeitform wird mit *to be* + *going to* + Verb (im Infinitiv) gebildet. Für Verneinungen benutzt man die Verneinungsformen von *to be*.

I'm going to visit	I'm not going to visit
he/she/it's going to visit	he/she/it isn't going to visit
we/you/they're going to visit	we/you/they aren't going to visit

Mit dem *going-future* spricht man über Pläne und Vorhaben.
Beispiel: *What are you **going to do** next Sunday? I'm **going to visit** a friend.*

to take part teilnehmen **survey** Umfrage, Befragung **married** verheiratet

[R/P] 5 Reading comprehension

Future visions

In the future many things will change. People already buy lots of things on the internet today. In the future we will buy even more. Shops will perhaps be only showrooms where we can see things and then order them online later at home. There will be supermarkets in the future, but they will be different. A computer screen on your trolley will show you where things are. You will put an electronic card in the computer on the trolley and it will give you a list of the things which you often buy. The computer will also contact your fridge at home and the fridge will inform you, "You need milk, sugar and eggs." There will not be any shop assistant anymore. Instead we will have electronic sales assistants. You ask a computer a question and it will give you an answer on the computer screen.

Read the text and sum up what it says about future shopping.

____

____

____

____

[P/I] 6 Your opinion

Discuss the advantages and disadvantages of the developments described in the text. How do you think shopping will be in the future? Present your ideas in class.

Skills: Mediation

'Mediation' means that you say in another language what a text is about. It does not mean that you translate word for word!

1 Mediation: English → German

Explain in German what the text above says about shopping in the future.

____

____

____

____

____

____

____

____

____

showroom	Ausstellungsraum	**fridge**	Kühlschrank	**to explain**	erklären
screen	Bildschirm	**development**	Entwicklung		

E Checking

[R/M] **1 Different customers**
Complete the sentences with words from the box and add the right type of customers.

compare • environmentally friendly • exactly • natural • take their time • usually • well-known

__________ customers like buying __________________________ **(umweltfreundlich)** products. They often buy goods made of __________ **(naturbelassen)** materials. __________ customers __________ **(vergleichen)** products with one another. They also __________ **(sich Zeit nehmen)** with shopping. Customers of __________ buy __________ **(bekannt)** products. They know __________ **(genau)** what they want to buy.

[P] **2 Plans for tomorrow**
Make sentences with 'going to'. Fill in the gaps.

1. "What ______________________ do tomorrow?" – "I ______________ unpack goods. Peter ______________ help me with it." 2. "______________________ be here tomorrow?" – "Yes, our boss ______________ meet a colleague from our branch in Toronto."

[R/P] **3 Future plans**
Tina has received an e-mail from an English friend. Write back and answer his questions.

```
Hi Tina,
Great that you have a job now.
But what will you do after your traineeship?
Will you look for a different job? Will you go
to a another country? Or will you work for the
same company?
Love, Jack
```

Dear Jack,

____

____

____

____

____

Ich kann jetzt ...

1. verschiedene Kundentypen und ihre Einkaufsgewohnheiten unterscheiden. ○○○
2. mich in Verkaufssituationen auf verschiedene Kundengruppen einstellen. ○○○
3. typische Merkmale verschiedener Geschäfte nennen. ○○○
4. Gründe nennen, weshalb Kunden bestimmte Geschäfte aufsuchen. ○○○

☺☺☺ = Kann ich schon!
☺☺ = Kann ich ein bisschen!
☺ = Kann ich bald!

gap Lücke **to receive** empfangen

Phrases: Addressing different customers

Adapting to different types of customers

The product is good for the environment.	Das Produkt ist gut für die Umwelt/ umweltverträglich.
It is biodegradable.	Es ist biologisch abbaubar.
Do you want to know what the product is made of?	Wollen Sie gerne wissen, woraus das Produkt gefertigt ist?
Are you interested in more information about the product?	Sind Sie an weiteren Informationen über das Produkt interessiert?
Would you like to try out another product?	Möchten Sie gerne ein anderes Produkt ausprobieren?
The product comes with a guarantee.	Das Produkt ist mit einer Garantie versehen.
I can speak more slowly if you wish.	Ich kann langsamer sprechen, falls Sie es wünschen.
I can repeat everything again.	Ich kann alles nochmals wiederholen.
I can say that again.	Ich kann das nochmal wiederholen.
I can show you how the product works.	Ich kann Ihnen zeigen, wie das Produkt funktioniert.
I can read the information out to you.	Ich kann Ihnen die Informationen vorlesen.
I can explain the difference to you.	Ich kann Ihnen den Unterschied erklären.
We have a special kids' zone.	Wir haben einen speziellen Kinderbereich.
We can take care of your children.	Wir können auf Ihre Kinder aufpassen.
Pardon?	Wie bitte?

Money 4

Am Ende dieser Unit kann ich ...

→ über die Verwendungsmöglichkeiten von Geld sprechen.
→ mit Kunden über Preise sprechen und Preisverhandlungen führen.
→ Probleme mit Kunden an der Kasse lösen.

Online Link 808225-0004

A Talking about money

[P] **1 At Harrods**
Describe the cartoon. (Tip: Harrods in London is one of the world's most famous department stores.)

[P] **2 Dealing with money**
What are the people doing? Use the words in the box and talk about the photos.

borrow money from • count money • pay money for • withdraw money from a cash dispenser

1

2

3

4

to deal (with)	(be)handeln	**to count**	zählen	**cash dispenser**	Geldautomat
to borrow	sich ausleihen	**to withdraw**	abheben		

B Goods and quantities

[R/P] **1 Listening: At the corner shop**

08 Listen to the dialogue and complete the shopping list for Steven.

1. one ________________ apples
2. a ____________ tomatoes
3. six ____________
4. three ____________ chocolate
5. five ________________ lemonade
6. two ________________ honey
7. a ____________ washing powder
8. ten ____________ toilet paper
9. two ______________ milk
10. a ____________ bread

At the corner shop

Assistant: Guten Morgen, was kann ich für Sie tun?
Steven: Excuse me. Do you speak English?
Assistant: Yes, I do. What can I do for you, Sir?
Steven: First of all, I'd like to buy one kilogram of apples. How much are they?
Assistant: They're € 2.50 a kilogram. Anything else?
Steven: Yes, a pound of tomatoes and some bananas, please.
Assistant: How many bananas would you like, Sir?
Steven: Six, please. And I need three bars of chocolate.
Assistant: The expensive ones or the cheap ones?
Steven: Is there a big difference in price?
Assistant: Yes, there is. The expensive ones cost twice as much as the cheap ones, Sir.
Steven: I'll take three bars of the cheaper chocolate, please.
Assistant: OK, Sir. Anything else?
Steven: Yes, five bottles of lemonade and two glasses of honey, please.
Assistant: A bottle of lemonade is € 0.95. Honey is on offer this week. You can have two for the price of one for € 4.00.
Steven: Excellent. Have you got any pineapples?
Assistant: Sorry, Sir. But we haven't got any left. They're completely sold out.
Steven: Well, I still need a packet of washing powder and ten rolls of toilet paper.
Assistant: No problem, Sir. Here you are. Anything else?
Steven: Yes, two litres of milk and a loaf of bread, please. Thank you. That's all for today. How much is it?
Assistant: That's € 28.95, Sir. Have you got exact change? I'm afraid I've got very few coins this morning.
Steven: Let me see. Yes, here you're.
Assistant: That's very kind of you, Sir. Do you need a carrier bag?
Steven: Yes, please.
Assistant: Here you are. Thank you for shopping with us.

quantity Menge
a bar of eine Tafel
difference Unterschied
expensive teuer
twice as much as zweimal so viel wie
honey Honig
pineapple Ananas
to have sth left etw. übrig haben
completely sold out vollständig ausverkauft
a packet of eine Packung
a roll of eine Rolle
a loaf of ein Laib
to have exact change es passend haben
carrier bag Tragetasche

[R/P] 2 Reading comprehension

Read the text on page 30 and answer the questions.

1. What problem does Steven have when the assistant greets him?

   ____

2. Does Steven buy the cheap or the expensive bars of chocolate?

   ____

3. How much is a bottle of lemonade?

   ____

4. Why can't Steven buy any pineapples?

   ____

[M] 3 Goods and quantities

Write down the following goods and quantities in English.

1. ______________ 2. ______________ 3. ______________ 4. ______________

Zahlen und Mengenangaben

Bei **Zahlen** ab 100, die mit einer ‚1' beginnen steht grundsätzlich *a* oder *one* vor der genannten Zahl.

1	one	15	fifteen	29	twenty-nine
2	two	16	sixteen	30	thirty
3	three	17	seventeen	40	forty
4	four	18	eighteen	50	fifty
5	five	19	nineteen	60	sixty
6	six	20	twenty	70	seventy
7	seven	21	twenty-one	80	eighty
8	eight	22	twenty-two	90	ninety
9	nine	23	twenty-three	100	a/one hundred
10	ten	24	twenty-four	101	a/one hundred and one
11	eleven	25	twenty-five	200	two hundred
12	twelve	26	twenty-six	201	two hundred and one
13	thirteen	27	twenty-seven	1000	a/one thousand
14	fourteen	28	twenty-eight	5251	five thousand two hundred and fifty-one

Mengenangaben werden in die Pluralform gesetzt, wenn mehrere Waren gekauft werden (z.B. *two bars of chocolate*). Die danach genannte Ware steht nur dann im Plural, wenn sie zählbar ist (z.B. *a packet of cigarettes*, ABER: *a packet of washing powder*). Weitere oft verwendete Mengenangaben sind: *a bottle of, a kilogram of, a litre of, a loaf of, a pound of, a roll of.*

C Talking about prices

[P/I] 1 Products and their prices

Write down how much each product costs. Then talk to a partner about the products and their prices.

→ See phrases on page 36.

£2.50 a kilo

1. ______________________________
____

one glass for £3.50, two glasses for £6.00

2. ______________________________
____

two for £2.80

3. ______________________________
____

£1.20 each

4. ______________________________
____

HIER UND DORT Preisauskünfte

Der Kunde/Die Kundin kann Fragen mit oder ohne *to do* stellen. Er/Sie könnte z.B. sagen: *"How much are the tomatoes?"* Bei nur einem gewünschten Pfund bzw. Kilo Tomaten würde er/sie dann sagen: *"How much is a kilogram/a pound of tomatoes?"* Mögliche Antworten sind: *"The tomatoes are € 2.99."* bzw. *"A/One kilogram/pound of tomatoes is € 2.99."* Wird die Frage mit *to do* gestellt, muss das Verb *cost* verwendet werden: *"How much do the tomatoes cost?"* oder *"How much does a kilo/a pound of tomatoes cost?"* Diese Frage wird mit *"The tomatoes cost € 2.99."* bzw. *"A/One kilo/pound of tomatoes costs € 2.99."* beantwortet. Nennt der Verkäufer/die Verkäuferin den Preis einer Ware muss ggf. eine Pluralform verwendet werden: *"The glass of marmalade costs one euro."*, ABER: *"A glass of honey costs two euros."*

[R/P] 2 Using adverbs and adjectives

Read the text on page 33. Complete the sentences with adverbs and adjectives from the text.

1. Fiona and Franziska go __________ to a department store. 2. The wallet was __________ overpriced before and now it looks as if it is a __________ bargain. 3. Franziska can get a __________ deal on toasters in the electrical appliances department. 4. Franziska's old toaster doesn't work __________ any more. 5. Fiona has read the leaflet __________, too. 6. Fiona and Franziska keep their eyes __________. 7. Fiona knows that Franziska can bargain __________ and thinks she is __________ clever.

wallet Geldbeutel
overpriced überteuert
electrical appliance Elektroartikel
a good deal ein gutes Angebot
leaflet Prospekt
to keep one's eyes open die Augen offen halten
to bargain handeln

In the leather goods department

Fiona and Franziska go quickly to a department store. Fiona wants to buy a new wallet.

Fiona: Look, this wallet is 30 percent off the regular price. The full price was originally 40 euros and now it's just 28 euros. I can save 12 euros!

Franziska: I think it was heavily overpriced before. Now it only looks as if it's a real bargain!

Fiona: I don't know. But maybe they'll put the price up again in a few days. I'll take it. It's exactly my taste.

Franziska: Just do it then, Fiona. By the way, in the electrical appliances department I can get a good deal on toasters. It was in their leaflet this morning. My old toaster doesn't work properly, as you know. If you don't mind, I'd like to go there.

Fiona: No problem. I've also read the leaflet carefully. You can get a brand-name product at the price of a no-name one.

Franziska: Yes, price reductions are no problem these days. You just have to keep your eyes open. Perhaps we can even get a further discount. OK?

Fiona: I know that you can bargain well, Franzi. You're really clever. So, let's go.

[R/P] **3 Adverb or adjective?**

Choose the correct word and cross out the wrong one.

1. Fiona shops **quick/quickly**.
2. Mr and Mrs Brown look **careful/carefully** at every product before they buy it.
3. Mohammed is a **nice/nicely** shop assistant.
4. Maria is **good/well** at English.
5. The toaster is a **real/really** bargain.
6. Paul is **particular/particularly** interested in computer games.

GRAMMAR SPOT Adjektive und Adverbien

	Adjektiv	Adverb
• Ein Adverb wird gebildet, indem *-ly* an das Adjektiv angehängt wird.	quick	quick**ly**
• Bei Adjektiven mit den Endungen *-y* wird das *-y* zu *-ily*, *-le* wird zu *-ly* und *-ic* wird zu *-ically*.	easy	eas**ily**
	simple	simp**ly**
	automatic	automat**ically**
• Das Adverb von *good* ist *well*.	good	**well**

Adjektive beschreiben Personen und Sachen.
Sie stehen meist vor einem Substantiv oder nach *to be*.
Beispiel: *a **big** shop* *The shop is **big**.*
Adverbien sagen etwas über Verben aus. Sie sagen uns, wie etwas passiert.
Beispiel: *Frank works **quickly**.*

→ Siehe Grammatikanhang auf S. 99.

leather goods Lederwaren
to be ... percent off ... Prozent weniger kosten
originally ursprünglich
to save sparen
taste Geschmack
if you don't mind wenn es dir/Ihnen nichts ausmacht
brand-name product Markenprodukt
reduction Ermäßigung
discount Nachlass, Rabatt
to cross out durchstreichen

D At the cash desk

[R/P] **1 Right or wrong?**

Look at the photos and dialogues. Then tick (✓) the correct boxes.

Situation A

- ☐ a) The cashier asks for some change from the customer.
- ☐ b) The customer has to pay more money for her goods.
- ☐ c) The customer has got exact change.

Situation B

- ☐ a) The cashier doesn't know what the customer wants.
- ☐ b) The customer finds a mistake on her receipt.
- ☐ c) The customer gets a repayment.

[P/I] **2 A mistake on the receipt**

Complete the conversation and act it out. → See phrases on page 36.

Customer	Shop assistant
Sorry, Sir/Madam, but I think ... on my receipt. →	Oh, ..., Sir/Madam.
I've bought ... but there are ... on the receipt. →	I'm ..., Sir/Madam. I'll ... Here's your ...
..., Sir/Madam. →	You're ... Thank you for ...

Skills: Doing internet research

When you are looking for information you can use a search engine (for example, Google). It is important to put in good key words in order to find the right information.

1 Using a search engine

Put the word 'Harrods' into a search engine. Find the homepage of Harrods and search for more information about its history. Then complete the following sentences.

Harrods was started in ____________ in London's ____________. Charles Harrod set up there as a ____________ grocer. In 1849 Harrod took over a small shop in the new district of ______________. Today Harrods is known all over the ____________.

2 Using an online dictionary

Check your spelling and any unknown words at: www.leo.de.

to cancel	stornieren	**key word**	Stichwort
repayment	Rückzahlung	**history**	Geschichte

E Checking

[R/P] **1 Listening: Pricing products**

09 Listen to the announcements in a supermarket. Then write down what each product costs.

1. ______________
2. ______________
3. ______________
4. ______________

[R/P] **2 Prepositions**

Put in the missing prepositions.

for • in • of (2x) • off • on • out

1. Frank buys three packets ______ the price ______ one.
2. The bananas are completely sold ______.
3. Two glasses ______ marmalade are ______ offer this week.
4. Some electrical appliances are 40 percent ______ the regular price.
5. There is a big difference ______ price.

[M] **3 Say it in English**

Put the sentences into English.

1. Ich bediene normalerweise nachmittags Kunden.
____
2. Ich sehe mir die Kunden sehr sorgfältig an.
____
3. Mein Chef ist nett und er spricht gut Englisch.
____
4. Natasha packt Ware sehr schnell aus.
____

Ich kann jetzt ...

1. über Verwendungsmöglichkeiten von Geld sprechen. ○○○
2. Mengenangaben für Produkte richtig anwenden. ○○○
3. Kunden die Preise von Produkten nennen und erfolgreich Preisverhandlungen führen. ○○○
4. Ich kann Probleme mit Kunden an der Kasse lösen. ○○○

☺☺☺ = Kann ich schon!
☺☺ = Kann ich ein bisschen!
☺ = Kann ich bald!

announcement Durchsage

Phrases: Dealing with money

Talking about goods and quantities

Would you like to buy a/one kilogram of/a pound of/a bar of/a bottle of/a litre of/a loaf of/a packet of/a roll of ...?	Hätten Sie gern ein Kilogramm/ein Pfund/eine Tafel/eine Flasche/einen Liter/einen Laib/eine Packung/eine Rolle ...?
I'm very sorry, but the product is completely sold out.	Es tut mir sehr leid, aber das Produkt ist vollständig ausverkauft.
We haven't got any ... left, I'm afraid.	Wir haben leider keine/n ... mehr da.

Talking about prices

The apples are/cost € 2.00 a kilogram.	Die Äpfel kosten 2,00 € das Kilo.
The product is excellent value for money.	Das Produkt ist sein Geld wert.
The goods are on offer this week.	Die Waren sind diese Woche im Angebot.
It's a real bargain.	Es ist ein wirkliches Schnäppchen.
You can save a lot of money.	Sie können eine Menge Geld sparen.
You can get a good deal on it.	Sie können dafür ein gutes Angebot bekommen.
You can even get a further discount.	Sie können sogar einen weiteren Nachlass/Rabatt erhalten.
The article is 30 percent off the regular price.	Der Artikel ist 30 Prozent günstiger als sonst.
We can give you big reductions.	Wir können Ihnen große Nachlässe gewähren.
I can't go down with the price any further.	Ich kann mit dem Preis nicht weiter heruntergehen.
You can buy two products for the price of one.	Sie können zwei Produkte für den Preis von einem kaufen.
There's a big difference in price.	Der Preisunterschied ist groß.
You can get one for free.	Sie bekommen einen/eine/eines umsonst.

Problems at the cash desk

Have you got exact change?	Haben Sie es passend?
Have you got 30 cents?	Haben Sie 30 Cent?
Sorry, Sir/Madam, but I don't have any change this morning.	Es tut mir leid, aber ich habe heute morgen kein Wechselgeld.
What's wrong with your receipt, Sir/Madam?	Was stimmt auf Ihrem Kassenzettel nicht?
Have you got your old receipt?	Haben Sie Ihren alten Kassenzettel noch?
Sorry for overcharging you.	Es tut mir leid, dass wir Ihnen zuviel berechnet haben.
I'll cancel your old receipt.	Ich werde Ihren alten Kassenzettel stornieren.
Here's your repayment and your new receipt.	Hier ist Ihre Rückerstattung und Ihr neuer Kassenzettel.

At the department store 5

Am Ende dieser Unit kann ich ...

→ Kunden beschreiben, wo sie die gewünschten Produkte finden.
→ Kunden den Weg in verschiedene Abteilungen weisen.
→ Personen und Sachen miteinander vergleichen.

Online Link 808225-0005

A Different floors

[P/I] **1 Where are the departments?**
Look at the photos and say on which floor the departments are.
Start like this: "The cosmetics department is on ..."

Tipp: Man sagt: ***in*** *the basement,*
ABER: ***on*** *the ground/first/second/top/... floor.*

children's wear • cosmetics • food • restaurant

1. Ground floor

2. Top floor

3. Basement

4. First floor

[R/P] **2 Listening: A new department store**
10
Listen to a radio programme. Write down on which floor certain products will be.
Then listen again and take notes about the reasons why products are on different floors.

	Food	Cosmetics	Children's wear
1. Where?			
2. Why?			

floor Stock(werk), Geschoss
children's wear Kinderbekleidung
basement Untergeschoss
ground floor Erdgeschoss
top floor Obergeschoss
to look forward to sich freuen auf
news Nachricht(en)

B Finding products

[R/P] 1 Reading comprehension

Read the dialogue between Tracy, a young tourist from the USA, and a shop assistant. Write down where the different products are.

1. lipstick: ______________________
2. eyeliner: ______________________
3. make-up: ______________________
4. nail polish: ______________________

In the cosmetics department

Tracy: Excuse me, could you help me, please? I'm looking for the cosmetics department.

Assistant: Certainly. Just follow me. I work in the cosmetics department and I'm just coming back from my lunch break. What exactly are you looking for?

Tracy: I need a new lipstick. It should be a bright colour.

Assistant: No problem. Let's go into the first aisle here. We have to go up to the end. Now, here they are, on the left: lipsticks in lots of different colours.

Tracy: Thank you very much. I'll take this one.

Assistant: Is there anything else I can do for you?

Tracy: Yes, Madam. I also need an eyeliner.

Assistant: They're next to the eye shadows. Right here in the second aisle round the corner.

Tracy: OK. By the way, I'll take some eye shadow, too. It makes my eyes more attractive, especially after a long night at the disco, you know?

Assistant: Yes, I know. I've got the same problem sometimes.

Tracy: I'd also like to buy some make-up.

Assistant: No, problem. It's at the beginning of the third aisle opposite the body lotion.

Tracy: Great. I always put on make-up in the mornings to look good. Now, there's only nail polish left.

Assistant: It's over there in the third aisle on the right between the nail polish remover and the nail scissors.

Tracy: Thanks for all your help.

Assistant: You're welcome, young lady.

[P/I] 2 Role play: Saying where the products are

Read the dialogue above with a partner. Then ask each other questions about where the products are.

Start like this: *Partner A:* Excuse me, where can I find ...?
Partner B: The ... are ...

→ See phrases on page 44.

lipstick	Lippenstift	**aisle**	Gang	**nail polish remover**	Nagellackentferner
lunch break	Mittagspause	**eye shadow**	Lidschatten		
bright	hell	**opposite**	gegenüber	**nail scissors**	Nagelschere

Ordnungszahlen

1st	first	6th	sixth	11th	eleventh	16th	sixteenth
2nd	second	7th	seventh	12th	twelfth	17th	seventeenth
3rd	third	8th	eighth	13th	thirteenth	19th	nineteenth
4th	fourth	9th	ninth	14th	fourteenth	18th	eighteenth
5th	fifth	10th	tenth	15th	fifteenth	20th	twentieth

C Finding different departments

[R] **1 At the information desk**

11 Read the questions 1.–4. and match them to the right answers a)–d). Draw lines.
Then listen to the conversations and check your answers.

Customers

1. Excuse me. Could you tell me where I can buy a doll?

2. Hello. Could you help me, please? We're having a barbecue this weekend. Where can I buy some sausages?

3. Sorry to disturb you. I'd like to buy some perfume but I can see only leather goods around me.

4. Excuse me. My son needs a new jacket. Where do I have to go?

Assistant

a) Please go downstairs to the supermarket in the basement.

b) Yes, of course. You just have to go to the toy department, Sir. You can take the lift round the corner up to the third floor, if you want.

c) You need to go to the children's wear department. Please take the escalator up to the second floor. The lift is out of order and must be repaired.

d) I can help you, Madam. Just stay on the ground floor. Please go straight on and you'll find the cosmetics behind the leather goods department.

information desk Informationsschalter	**toy** Spielzeug	**out of order** außer Betrieb
doll Puppe	**barbecue** Grillparty	**to repair** reparieren
downstairs (nach) unten	**lift** Aufzug	**to stay** bleiben
	escalator Rolltreppe	**straight on** geradeaus

[R/M] **2 Listening: Finding the way**
11 Listen again and complete the following sentences.

Please (1) ________________ **(nach unten gehen)** to the supermarket (2) ________________ **(im Untergeschoss)**. The (3) ____________________ **(Spielzeugabteilung)** is on the third floor. You can take the (4) ____________________ **(Fahrstuhl)** if you want. You have to take the (5) ____________________ **(Rolltreppe)** to go to the children's wear department. The lift is (6) ________________________ **(außer Betrieb)**. The cosmetics department is (7) __________________ **(hinter)** this one. Just go (8) ______________________ **(geradeaus)**.

D Making comparisons

[R/P] **1 A present for a friend**
Fiona has received an e-mail from her friend Susan. Read the text and write an answer. Use the words in the box.

best • cheaper • more beautiful • more expensive • prettiest

Hi, Fiona,
I miss you a lot and hope you're fine. Please do me a favour, as you're my best friend, Fiona. I've heard that they have some really fashionable T-shirts in Germany that look prettier and more stylish than those in Britain. As you know, they are also more expensive here in Britain than in Germany. If you find some cheaper ones which look at least as stylish as the ones I always wear, then please BUY them. I'll give you the money when you're back. Promise!
Love, Susan

____
____
____
____
____
____
____
____
____

favour	Gefallen	**at least**	wenigstens	**promise**	Versprechen

GRAMMAR SPOT Steigerung von Adjektiven

Einsilbige Adjektive werden im Englischen mit *-er* und *-est* gesteigert, zweisilbige Adjektive, die auf *-y* enden mit *-ier* und *-iest*. Bei Vergleichen benutzt man *than* (= als).
Beispiele: *He is **older than** Frank. He is **the oldest**. Susan is **prettier than** Tina. Dana is **the prettiest**.*

Die meisten anderen zweisilbigen Adjektive und alle mehrsilbigen Adjektive, werden mit *more* und *most* gesteigert.
Beispiele: *The house is **more modern** than Paul's. Jackie's house is **the most modern** one in Brighton. My car is **more expensive** than Melanie's. Bob's car is **the most expensive**.*

Bei Vergleichen von Personen und Sachen verwendet man *as ... as* oder *not as ... as*.
Beispiele: *Conny's trolley is **as big as** Frank's. Sean's stereo is **not as good as** Naomi's.*

Einige Adjektive haben unregelmäßige Steigerungsformen:

good	**better**	**best**	bad	**worse**	**worst**
much/many	**more**	**most**	little	**less**	**least**

Beispiel: *This jam is **the least expensive**.*

[P/I] **2 Comparing products at Marks & Spencer**
First write down three adjectives for each bag. Then work with a partner and describe the bags. Compare the bags and decide which one you would like to buy and say why.
Start like this: "The bag on the left is ..."

1. ______________________
____
____

2. ______________________
____
____

3. ______________________
____
____

HIER UND DORT Warenhäuser in Großbritannien

1. Das berühmteste und exklusivste britische Kaufhaus **Harrods** befindet sich im Südwesten Londons. Es zählt keineswegs zu den preisgünstigsten Einkaufsmöglichkeiten, dennoch steht es allen Menschen offen und wird von vielen Touristen besucht. Allerdings gibt es ein paar Beschränkungen und so ist beispielsweise das Betreten des Kaufhauses in stark auffallender Kleidung (z. B. Punk, Heavy Metal) verboten.
2. **Marks & Spencer** ist als Warenhauskonzern in Großbritannien sehr bekannt und mit ca. 300 Geschäften vertreten. Er gilt als das profitabelste Einzelhandelsunternehmen Europas. Anders als viele deutsche Warenhäuser bietet Marks & Spencer kein umfassendes Sortiment an, sondern beschränkt sich auf Bekleidung, Nahrungsmittel und Haushaltswaren. Ca. 16 Millionen Kunden kaufen dort jede Woche ein.

[P] 3 Explaining things in different words

Sometimes you may not remember certain words in English. Then you should use other words to say the same thing. Use the verbs in brackets and rewrite the sentences in simple language.

Example: Can I borrow some money from you? (to give) → Can you give me some money?

1. How much does a pound of tomatoes cost? **(to be)**

   ____

2. This wallet is heavily overpriced. **(to cost)**

   ____

3. Could you tell me where I can buy some toilet paper? **(to know)**

   ____

4. Can you do me a favour, please? **(to help)**

   ____

Skills: British and American English

Certain words are different in British English and American English. Sometimes just the spelling is different, but some words are completely different. In your dictionary British and American English words are usually marked as BrE or Brit and as AmE or Am.

1 Different spelling

Write the sentences in American English. Use a dictionary, if necessary.

1. My mum is a teacher.

   ____

2. Our house is near the city centre.

   ____

3. Can you do me a favour, please?

   ____

2 Different words

Fill in the missing words and complete the list. Then check your answers with the help of a dictionary.

British English	American English	German
shop assistant		Verkäufer/in
	vacation	
biscuit		Keks
	elevator	Aufzug
	fall	Herbst
flat		Wohnung

to remember sich erinnern (an) **bracket** Klammer

E Checking

[R/P] 1 Retail crossword

Find the right words and fill in the crossword.

Across:

1. It moves up and down between different floors.
3. You can put your money in it.
5. It is a stair and it moves.
10. In most department stores the food department is in the ...
11. Another word for lipsticks, body lotions, etc.

Down:

2. I usually withdraw money from the cash ...
4. Please go upstairs, don't go ...
6. The ... floor is below the first floor.
7. The highest floor in a building is the ... floor.
8. When you work hard, you have to take a ... sometimes.
9. On the other side.

[R/P] 2 Comparisons

Find the correct words in each sentence and underline them.

1. The nail polish is **expensive/more expensive** than the lipstick.
2. The new department store is **more modern/most modern** than the old one.
3. Susan's English is **the worst/worse** than Verena's.
4. This is the **biggest/bigger** supermarket in our town.
5. Ulrike is **as nice as/as nice than** Julia.

[M] 3 Mediation

Anja has received a letter from Tom. Sum it up in German. Write in your exercise book.

Hi, Anja,

How are you? You know, I've just come back from a weekend in Paris. It was fantastic. What I liked best was going shopping there. It was much more interesting than here in Manchester. I went to the biggest department store in Paris and bought myself some cool CDs. Then I went up to the top floor and had lunch in the restaurant. The food was much better and less expensive than English food.

What about you? What did you do last weekend?

Love, Tom

Ich kann jetzt ...

1. die Stockwerke eines Warenhauses benennen.
2. Gründe angeben, warum bestimmte Produkte in unterschiedlichen Stockwerken zu finden sind.
3. Kunden sagen, wo sie Produkte finden können und den Weg in verschiedene Abteilungen weisen.
4. Personen und Sachen miteinander vergleichen.

(three smileys) = Kann ich schon!
(two smileys) = Kann ich ein bisschen!
(one smiley) = Kann ich bald!

to move bewegen

Phrases: At a department store

Asking for products

Excuse me, could you tell me where I can find ...?	Entschuldigen Sie, könnten Sie mir sagen, wo ich ... finden kann?
Sorry to disturb you, but could you show me where ... is/are?	Es tut mir leid Sie zu stören, aber könnten Sie mir zeigen, wo ... ist/sind?
Excuse me, Sir/Madam but I need your help to find ...	Entschuldigen Sie, aber ich benötige Ihre Hilfe, um ... zu finden.
Excuse me, where is/are ...?	Entschuldigen Sie, wo ist/sind ...?

Showing the way to different departments

The product you are looking for is in the basement/on the ground floor/first/second/third/top floor.	Das Produkt nach dem Sie suchen befindet sich im Untergeschoss/Erdgeschoss/ersten/zweiten/dritten/obersten Stock.
Please take the lift to the ... floor.	Bitte nehmen Sie den Aufzug in den ... Stock.
You can also take the stairs up/down to the ... floor.	Sie können auch die Treppe hoch/runter in den ... Stock nehmen.
You can also go upstairs to the ... department.	Sie können auch nach oben in die ... Abteilung gehen.
Just go downstairs to the ... floor.	Gehen Sie einfach die Treppe nach unten in den ... Stock.
The toy/sports/... department is ...	Die Spielzeug/Sport/...abteilung ist ...

Making comparisons

Paul is older/happier/more intelligent/... than Bob.	Paul ist älter/glücklicher/intelligenter/... als Bob.
Paul is the oldest/happiest/most intelligent/... guy.	Paul ist der älteste/glücklichste/intelligenteste/... Kerl.
The new school building is more modern than the old one.	Das neue Schulgebäude ist moderner als das alte.
He is the best/worst shop assistant in our department store.	Er ist der beste/schlechteste Verkäufer in unserem Kaufhaus.
The sausages are (not) as delicious as the sandwich.	Die Würstchen sind (nicht) so schmackhaft wie der Sandwich.

Sales promotion 6

Am Ende dieser Unit kann ich …

→ Werbematerial verstehen und entwerfen.
→ Radiowerbung verstehen.
→ Interesse an Produkten erkennen und richtig darauf reagieren.
→ Kunden produktbezogene Fragen beantworten.

Online Link 808225-0006

A The history of a company

[R] **1 Listening: Coca-Cola on promotion tour**

12 Listen to Tanja Kugler and put the pictures in the right order. Write the numbers 1–8 in the boxes below the pictures.

Tanja works for the public relations department of the Coca-Cola company in Germany. Today she is opening a sales promotion week. She is talking about the history of the company.

Asa Candler

Dr John S. Pemberton

The original Coca-Cola logo designed by Frank Robinson

Coca-Cola in bottles

Coca-Cola in cans

Coca-Cola in China

sales promotion	Verkaufsförderung	**can**	Dose	**state**	Staat
public relations	Öffentlichkeitsarbeit	**to invent**	erfinden	**businessman**	Geschäftsmann
		pharmacist	Apotheker/in		
		famous	berühmt		

B Planning a product promotion

[R/P] **1 Reading comprehension**

Your boss has given you the flyer for an energy drink that you are going to offer to customers in a promotion week. A British company plans to introduce the drink in Germany.

Strawberry Super Energy Drink

Taste and enjoy it! You will get the power you need to cope with your daily challenges! You can't resist it. You are invited to be one of the first customers to celebrate the launch of this exclusive new product with us from 18 June to 22 June.

Every customer who drinks a glass of Strawberry Super Energy Drink and tells us what he/she thinks about the product will automatically take part in our competition and can win a prize.

Just tick one of the three boxes on the back of the flyer and include your name and address. Then give it to a shop assistant. You and a partner of your choice could become one of the six lucky winners of a weekend trip to Paris. Stay in a five-star hotel and take € 1,000 with you for an exclusive shopping tour.

Don't miss your chance!

Read the flyer and answer the questions.

1. What is special about this product?

____

2. What do customers have to do to win a prize?

____

____

3. What can customers win in the competition?

____

____

____

[P/I] **2 Designing a poster**

Find partners who work in the same or a similar branch as you. Together design a poster for a new product that you are planning to sell soon. Present your poster in class and say what is special about the product.

→ See phrases on page 52.

flyer	Werbeblatt	**challenge**	Herausforderung	**launch**	Start
to introduce	einführen	**to resist**	widerstehen	**competition**	Wettbewerb
to cope with	fertig werden mit	**to invite**	einladen	**prize**	Preis(gewinn)
		to celebrate	feiern	**five-star hotel**	5-Sterne-Hotel

C Convincing and binding customers

[R/P] **1 Reading comprehension**

The company Mobile Solutions is planning a new mobile phone campaign for British soldiers in Germany. They have asked you to do some promotion for it in your shop. First read the background information. Then match the sentence parts and draw lines.

1. In 1973 engineers in the USA
2. The first portable phones were heavy
3. In the 1980s the production of
4. In today's money
5. The first commercial portable phone
6. Today many people

a) have a mobile phone.
b) the first commercial portable phone started.
c) the first commercial phone cost about $ 4,000.
d) didn't have text messaging.
e) invented the first portable mobile phone.
f) and weighed more than a kilogram.

Mobile phones – A success story

In the early 1970s a team of engineers in the USA invented the first modern mobile phone. In 1973 the phone was demonstrated for the first time, and one of the inventors made a phone call from a street in New York. People stopped and looked at him because they had never seen something like this before: A man with a phone in the street! About ten years later the production of the first commercial portable phones started. These phones were very simple and they didn't have any text messaging or cameras. They were also heavy – over a kilogram. Compared with later mobile phones, they were expensive: In today's money, the price of one of the first phones was about $ 4,000. Since then an increasing number of people have been using a mobile phone at work and in their daily life all over the world. Indeed, many people today think that they can't live without a mobile phone anymore.

to convince	überzeugen	**engineer**	Ingenieur/in	**text messaging**	Textmitteilung
to bind	(an sich) binden	**production**	Herstellung	**to weigh**	wiegen
mobile phone	Handy	**to weigh**	wiegen	**to increase**	zunehmen
campaign	Kampagne	**to demonstrate**	*hier:* vorführen		
background	Hintergrund				

[P/I] **2 Your mobile phone**

Think about your first mobile phone and answer the questions. Fill in your part of the table first. Then ask a partner and complete the table. Use the simple past.

1. When did you get your first mobile phone?
2. Which functions did it have (text messaging, MP3 player, ...)?
3. Who did you call first (a friend/your mum ...)?

You	Your partner
1. I got	1. He/She got

GRAMMAR SPOT Das *simple past*

Das *simple past* wird verwendet, um Ereignisse in der Vergangenheit zu schildern, die jetzt abgeschlossen sind. Regelmäßige Verben bilden das *simple past* mit *-ed*. Unregelmäßige Verben haben Sonderformen. Verneinungen bildet man mit *didn't*, Fragen mit *did*. Nach *did* und *didn't* steht immer die Grundform.

	I/He/She/It/We/You/They	start**ed**	**went**
	I/He/She/It/We/You/They	**didn't** start	**didn't** go
Did	I/he/she/it/we/you/they	**start**?	**go**?

→ Siehe Grammatikanhang auf S. 93.

Das Verb *to be* hat zwei Formen im *simple past*. Es bildet Fragen und Verneinungen ohne *did/didn't*.

I/He/She/It	**was/wasn't**
We/You/They	**were/weren't**

Beispiel: *When **was** your birthday? Where **were** you last week?*
Typische Zeitangaben in Verbindung mit dem *simple past* sind: *ago, in 1990, last week, then.*

[R] **3 Listening: Advertising on the radio**

13

Mobile Solutions also advertises on the British radio. Listen and tick (✓) the right boxes.

1. The new mobile phone
   - ☐ a) is delivered with an earphone.
   - ☐ b) has a flat rate for calls to Britain.
   - ☐ c) is a special offer for soldiers stationed in Britain.
2. The new mobile phone is called
   ☐ a) 'Mum'. ☐ b) 'Home'. ☐ c) 'Friends'.
3. The special offer includes
   - ☐ a) free calls to the USA every day.
   - ☐ b) a flate rate for calls in Germany at the weekend.
   - ☐ c) a monthly flat rate for using the internet and phoning to Britain.

to advertise	Werbung machen	**flat rate**	einheitlicher Kostensatz	**to include**	beinhalten
				period of time	Zeitraum
to deliver	(aus)liefern	**soldier**	Soldat/in	**angry**	wütend
earphone	Ohrhörer	**to station**	stationieren	**bill**	Rechnung

[R/P] **4 Promotions in the store**

Read the dialogues and find out if the customers are interested, unsure or not interested. Underline the correct answer.

1. The first customer is **interested/unsure/not interested** in the offer.
2. The second customer is **interested/unsure/not interested**.
3. The third customer is **interested/unsure/not interested**.

Dialogue 1

Assistant: Good morning. Can I help you?

Customer: Yes, you can. I listened to the radio advert about your new mobile phone this morning. May I have a closer look at it?

Assistant: Yes, of course. It's stylish, easy to use and has a big screen for comfortable internet research.

Customer: May I try and call my son in Bristol?

Assistant: No problem, Madam. Here you are.

Dialogue 2

Assistant: Hello, Madam. We have a very attractive mobile phone on offer. Why don't you call your family in Britain for free?

Customer: I know you and your offers. Nothing is for free. I've never had a mobile and don't want one either.

Assistant: I see, Madam. Have a nice day.

Dialogue 3

Assistant: Excuse me, Sir. Are you interested in more information about our mobile phones?

Customer: Well, I can't really decide. Please give me a leaflet about the products and I'll read it at home. Maybe I'll come back tomorrow.

Assistant: No problem, Sir. Here you are. If you have got any questions, please feel free to contact us again.

Customer: That sounds good. Thank you, Sir.

[P] **5 An e-mail from a customer**

A customer has written an e-mail to your boss. Complete the text with words from the box. Use the simple past.

be • buy • call • come • enter • have • inform • offer • send

Dear Sir or Madam

Last week I (1) ______________ your shop and (2) ______________ the new mobile phone that you (3) ______________ in your campaign. Your shop assistant (4) ________ very nice and (5) ______________ me about all the details. When I (6) ______________ home, I (7) ____________ my wife in Manchester and (8) ______________ a long conversation with her. Yesterday I even (9) ______________ her an e-mail from my mobile. It (10) ______________ so easy! I hope you will advertise more products in the future.

Yours faithfully
Simon Berry

unsure unsicher

[M] **6 Mediation**

Sum up the e-mail on page 49 for a colleague who doesn't speak English.

____

____

____

____

____

[P/I] **7 Role play: Product promotion**

Form groups and develop dialogues between shop assistants and customers. You can choose ideas from the box or think of a promotion in your own shop.

- Agree on a product that you want to promote.
- Collect benefits of the product that make it special for the customers.
- Identify the target group (teenagers/...).
- Practise dialogues between customers and shop assistants.
- Present your role plays in class.

→ See phrases on page 52.

diet drinks • glittering lipsticks • outdoor jackets

HIER UND DORT Kundenbindung

Kunden an sich zu binden ist eine wichtige Voraussetzung, um mit einem Geschäft erfolgreich zu sein. Dem Service fällt dabei eine Schlüsselrolle zu. Die Studie einer britischen Unternehmensberatung zeigt, dass der Service den deutsche Unternehmen bieten im internationalen Vergleich führend ist. Deutsche Kunden sind zwar nicht leichter zufrieden zu stellen als Kunden im Ausland, sie erhalten aber den besseren Service.

Skills: Describing a picture

When you describe a picture, first describe what you see in the foreground and background, on the left and the right. Then say what people and places look like.

1 Where things and people are

Look at the photo on page 47 and complete the sentences.

1. ______________ there is a young man with his girlfriend. 2. ______________ there is a shop which is selling fruit. 3. ______________ there are more people and some houses.

2 Details

Look at the photo on page 47 again and underline the right words.

The couple in the foreground are **shouting/smiling** and look **angry/happy**. The young woman is wearing a **blue dress/white T-shirt.** The shop assistant in the background has **long/short** hair. The elderly person on the right is carrying a **blue bag/red rucksack**.

3 Your turn

Choose a picture from your book and describe it to a partner.

to agree sich einigen **target group** Zielgruppe **foreground** Vordergrund

D Checking

[R/P] 1 Prepositions

Put in the correct preposition. Use the words from the box.

after • for (2x) • to • with

We have prepared a flyer (1) ________ promote an energy drink that helps you to cope (2) ________ your daily challenges. It is (3) ________ people who want to stay fit. Customers can ask (4) ________ a glass of the drink. (5) ________ a few minutes they will feel great.

[P] 2 Asking questions

Make questions and ask for the underlined parts of the sentences.

1. Katharina worked at a fashion shop in Braunschweig last year.

   ____

2. We went to Australia last summer.

   ____

3. My mother bought five bananas at the supermarket.

   ____

4. We offered a flat rate because it makes our offer more attractive.

   ____

[P] 3 Word order

Find the right order and put the verbs in the simple past.

1. want/Mr Winter/week/the sales promotion/to open/on Monday

   ____

2. in contact/stay/home/family/We/back/with/our

   ____

3. Paris/last year/win/We/trip/to/a

   ____

4. drink/They/the/other/country/sell/no/in

   ____

Ich kann jetzt ...

1. eine Firmengeschichte nachvollziehen.
2. den Inhalt von Werbematerialien wiedergeben.
3. ein Poster für eine Werbeaktion entwerfen.
4. Produktwerbung im Radio verstehen.
5. bei Kunden Interesse an Produkten erkennen, richtig darauf reagieren und produktbezogene Fragen beantworten.

☺☺☺ = Kann ich schon!

☺☺ = Kann ich ein bisschen!

☺ = Kann ich bald!

Phrases: Product promotion

Planning a product promotion

Mrs Kugler is opening a sales promotion week.	Frau Kugler eröffnet gerade eine Verkaufsförderungswoche.
We are planning a product promotion/new campaign.	Wir planen eine Produktwerbung/neue Kampagne.
I will do some promotion for the product.	Ich werde Werbung für das Produkt machen.
We can advertise our product on the radio.	Wir können im Radio für unser Produkt Werbung machen.
We ask assistants from the public relations department to help us.	Wir bitten Mitarbeiter, aus der Abteilung für Öffentlichkeitsarbeit uns zu helfen.
We will design a poster for a new product.	Wir werden ein Plakat für ein neues Produkt entwerfen.
We want to celebrate the launch of the product.	Wir möchten den Verkaufsstart des Produktes feiern.
I can give you some background information about the product.	Ich kann Ihnen einige Hintergrundinformationen zum Produkt geben.
You can take part in a competition.	Sie können an einem Preisausschreiben/ Wettbewerb teilnehmen.
You can win a prize.	Sie können einen Preis gewinnen.
You can try our products.	Sie können unsere Produkte ausprobieren.
Here's our flyer for the new energy drink.	Hier ist unser Werbeblatt/Flyer für den neuen Energiedrink.

Explaining products

Excuse me, are you interested in more information about our new product?	Entschuldigung, sind Sie an weiteren Informationen über unser neues Produkt interessiert?
You can try our mobile phone, if you want.	Sie können unser Mobiltelefon gerne ausprobieren, wenn Sie möchten.
If you have any questions, please feel free to contact us again.	Falls Sie Fragen haben, können Sie sich mit uns jederzeit wieder in Verbindung setzen.

Special sales situations 7

Am Ende dieser Unit kann ich …

- → Kunden den richtigen Umgang mit Produkten erläutern und Pflegehinweise geben.
- → auf Kundeneinwände angemessen reagieren.
- → im Laden geltende Regeln und Vorschriften erläutern.
- → verärgerte Kunden beruhigen und ihnen Problemlösungen anbieten.

Online Link 808225-0007

A Handling goods

[R/P] **1 Customers handling goods**

Look at the photos and decide if customers are allowed to touch the products shown (✓) or not (×). Then choose the right sentence and write the number in the box next to the photo.

1. Customers are allowed to touch it and study the label. • 2. You can try it out and find out how it smells. • 3. You are not allowed to touch it because it is fragile. • 4. The customer can try them on and see if they fit. • 5. You must call a shop assistant who can show you how it works. • 6. You are allowed to touch it and feel the material.

☐ a computer

☐ a carpet

☐ a bottle of wine

☐ a bottle of perfume

☐ clothes

☐ a vase

to handle	handhaben	**to smell**	riechen	**sample**	Muster
to be allowed to	dürfen	**fragile**	zerbrechlich		
to touch	anfassen	**carpet**	Teppich(boden)		

B Giving instructions

> **Tipp**
> *must* = müssen, *mustn't* = nicht dürfen

[R/P] 1 Dos and don'ts

Complete the sentences with verbs from the box.

1. If an elderly lady takes goods from the shelves she ________________ unpack them.
2. When customers ask the assistant questions their children ________________ be quiet.
3. In difficult situations you ________________ become nervous.
4. At the cash desk customers ________________ pay by credit card.

> *isn't allowed to • must • mustn't • don't have to*

[P] 2 Dealing with difficult situations

What would you say to customers in these situations? Use the words in brackets.

Example: A customer is pressing buttons on a mobile phone. (aren't allowed/go wrong) → "Excuse me, Sir, but you aren't allowed to do that. It could go wrong. But I can show you how it works if you want."

→ See phrases on page 60.

1. A customer is touching soft fruit. **(aren't allowed to touch/go off)**

   ____

   ____

2. A customer is touching a carpet. **(are allowed to touch/feel the material)**

   ____

   ____

3. A customer is reading a travel guide in a book store. **(may look/show more guides)**

   ____

   ____

[P/I] 3 Rules at school

Think about the rules at your school and talk to a partner about them.

Start like this: At school, I must ... I don't have to ... We mustn't ... We're allowed to ...

[P] 4 Explaining care instructions

Match the symbols to the instructions and draw lines.

1. 
2. 
3. 
4. 
5. 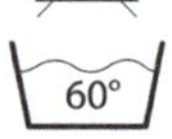

6. 

a) You can wash the clothes in the washing machine at 60°.
b) You should wash this piece of clothing by hand.
c) You mustn't bleach this product.
d) You are allowed to iron this piece of clothing with low heat.
e) You must protect this product against humidity.
f) Extremely flammable! You must protect it from sunlight.

credit card	Kreditkarte	**rule**	Regel	**heat**	Hitze
button	Knopf	**care instruction**	Pflegehinweis	**flammable**	entflammbar
to go wrong	schiefgehen	**to bleach**	bleichen	**to protect**	schützen
to go off	schlecht werden	**to iron**	bügeln	**humidity**	Feuchtigkeit
travel guide	Reiseführer				

GRAMMAR SPOT Modale Hilfsverben

Mit *must/have to, mustn't* und *don't/doesn't have to* wird ausgedrückt, was man tun muss, nicht tun darf und nicht zu tun braucht.

I	**must**	**mustn't**
he/she/it	**must**	**mustn't**
we/you/they	**must**	**mustn't**
I	**have to**	**don't have to**
he/she/it	**has to**	**doesn't have to**
we/you/they	**have to**	**don't have to**

must/have to = müssen — *I **must/have to** go to school five days a week.*
mustn't = nicht dürfen — *I **mustn't** smoke in this room.*
don't have to = nicht brauchen — *I **don't have to go** to school on Sundays.*

→ Siehe Grammatikanhang auf S. 96.

C Explaining rules and regulations

[R/P/I] **1 Role play: Explaining rules to customers**

Sometimes customers do not keep to the rules in your shop. Work with a partner and explain the rules politely to each other. Use the phrases in the box.

I'm really sorry, Sir/Madam, but ... • Excuse me, but ... • Unfortunately I have to tell you that ... • Sorry Sir/Madam, but you aren't allowed to ... • You mustn't ... • You must/have to ... • You don't have to ...

→ See phrases on page 60.

1. Two boys want to buy alcohol and cigarettes. They are too young to buy these products. → Customers under the age of 17 are not allowed to buy cigarettes and alcohol.
2. A couple enters a home-entertainment shop with their bags. → Customers must leave their bags at the information desk. You can pick them up after shopping.
3. A customer enters a fashion shop with an ice cream. → Customers mustn't bring any food into the shop.
4. A customer smokes in the non-smoking area of a restaurant. → Customers are allowed to smoke in special smoking areas.
5. An old lady touches clothes with dirty fingers. → You have to keep the products in good condition.
6. A customer walks with his dog through the aisles of a supermarket. → You are not allowed to bring pets inside. Ask our assistants and they will look after your pet while you go shopping.
7. A customer wants to pay for some sweets by credit card. → Purchases under €15 mustn't be paid by credit card.

regulation Vorschrift	**unfortunately** leider	**condition** Zustand
to keep sich halten (an)	**smoking area** Raucherzone	**pet** Haustier
polite höflich	**dirty** dreckig	**purchase** Einkauf

[R/I] **2 Regulations in your shop**
Which regulations do you have in your shop?
Work in groups and explain them to each other.

→ See phrases on page 60.

D Dealing with customer complaints

[R/P] **1 Customers complaining**
Read the description of two situations in which customers are complaining.
Complete the sentences with the words given in the boxes.

accepts • appreciates • button • exception • exchange • gardening • information desk • point • purchase • receipt • replacement • returns • ruined • suggestion • voucher

Situation 1: At the DIY-shop

A customer bought a pair of gloves for (1) ______________. He is very upset because they were (2) ______________ after two hours of work in the garden. The shop assistant makes a (3) ______________. He offers to (4) ______________ the gloves and gives him a (5) ______________ for € 10. The customer (6) ______________ the offer and (7) ______________ the service.

Situation 2: At the toys and games department

A woman enters a shop with a doll and a (1) ______________. She has just come from the (2) ______________ and wants to exchange the doll. She is angry because the doll doesn't speak when you press the (3) ______________. The shop assistant sees her (4) ______________ and wants to know when she bought the doll. The shop accepts (5) ______________ within two weeks after the (6) ______________. He wants to give a (7) ______________ for it but it is now three weeks after the purchase. However, the shop assistant makes an (8) ______________.

[R/I] **2 Role play: Talking to a dissatisfied customer**
Work with a partner. One of you is a shop assistant, the other is a customer. Use the situations in exercise 1 and the phrases below. Then change roles.

Shop assistant	**Customer**
How can I help you?	I have a complaint to make.
What exactly happened?	I'm very upset.
The problem is easy to solve.	I want to report a problem.
I can offer you a replacement.	I'll accept your offer.
Let me make you a suggestion.	That's very kind of you.
I can see your point.	Thanks a lot.
That can happen sometimes, but ...	I really appreciate your excellent service.

→ See phrases on page 60.

complaint	Beschwerde	**return**	Rückgabe	**upset**	aufgebracht
to appreciate	schätzen	**to ruin**	ruinieren	**to see a point**	einen Standpunkt verstehen
exception	Ausnahme	**suggestion**	Vorschlag	**dissatisfied**	unzufrieden
to exchange	(um)tauschen	**voucher**	Gutschein	**to solve**	lösen
replacement	Ersatz	**glove**	Handschuh		

[R/P] 3 Reading comprehension

25 Greenhill Road
Lancaster
LA 11YQ

12 May 2009

Rimpo Electronics
7 Castle Park
Lancaster
LC 31 XT

Dear Mr Schwarz,

My complaint of 10 May 2009

I have been a loyal customer of your shop for many years. Today I must praise the reaction of one of your assistants to my complaint last week.

I am a fan of Heavy Metal music and I bought myself a new CD of my favourite group in your shop about a week ago. Unfortunately, the CD had scratches which I saw only when I arrived home. The next day I went back to your shop and explained the situation to one of your shop assistants. He took a new CD from the shelf and exchanged the old one without asking any more questions. Additionally, he gave me a voucher for a 10 % discount on any products that I buy in your shop within the next six months.

I would like to thank you for your excellent service. I will certainly recommend your shop. Please inform your friendly shop assistants about this letter, too.

Your loyal customer,

Richard Johnson

Read the letter to the owner of a home-entertainment shop. Then answer the questions.

1. Why did the customer write a letter to the shop owner?

____

____

2. What did the customer buy?

____

____

3. When did the customer buy the CD and what did he see at home?

____

____

4. How did the shop assistant react when the customer wanted to have a replacement?

____

____

5. What did the customer ask the shop owner to do at the end of the letter?

____

____

to praise loben **scratch** Kratzer **to recommend** empfehlen

E Convincing upset customers

[R/P] **1 Listening: Dealing with an upset customer**
14 A customer is making a complaint. Listen to the dialogue and complete the sentences.

1. The customer is upset because ______
2. In the future the customer is going to ______
3. The manager offers the customer ______
4. The customer accepts the suggestion but only if ______

[M] **2 Mediation**
Translate the sentences into German.

1. An upset customer is a customer who is unhappy.
   ______
2. A cafeteria is a place where you can buy food and drinks.
   ______
3. The brochure which came from England was very interesting.
   ______

GRAMMAR SPOT Relativsätze → Siehe Grammatikanhang auf S. 99.

Wir verwenden *who, which* und *where,* um Menschen, Sachen und Orte genauer zu beschreiben: *who* für Personen, *which* für Sachen und *where* für Orte.
Beispiele: *A shop assistant is a person/someone* ***who*** *... A computer is a machine* ***which*** *...*
A supermarket is a place ***where*** *...*

Skills: Listening
When you are hearing a text for the first time, you should concentrate on the content. Don't try to understand the details yet. When you are listening for a second time, take notes of important information.

1 A telephone call
When a person is calling from abroad, listen carefully. Ask about things that you haven't understood. Put the following phrases into English and use the verbs in the box.

to get right • to repeat • to spell

1. Können Sie das bitte für mich wiederholen?
   ______
2. Habe ich das richtig verstanden?
   ______
3. Es tut mir leid, aber ich verstehe gerade nicht was Sie sagen.
   ______
4. Könnten Sie das bitte für mich buchstabieren?
   ______

to calm down beruhigen	**from abroad** aus dem Ausland
to lose verlieren	**to get right** (richtig) verstehen
inconvenience Unannehmlichkeit	**to repeat** wiederholen
content Inhalt	

F Checking

[R/P] **1 Retail crossword**

Fill in the right words.

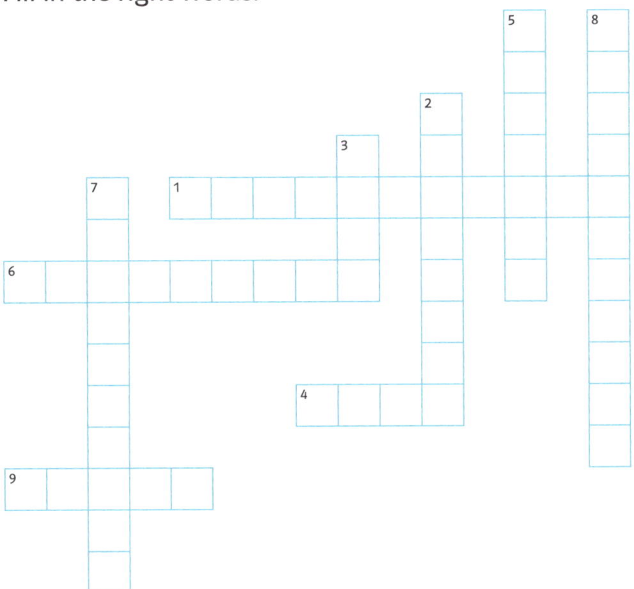

Across:
1. Information that tells you how to do or use something.
4. It tells you what you are allowed or not allowed to do.
6. If something burns easily it is ...
9. Something that you can win in a competition.

Down:
2. When you give something and get something similar back.
3. If you don't have to pay for something, then you get it for ...
5. A product which breaks easily is ...
7. Someone who makes medicines in a shop or hospital.
8. A man who works in business.

[R/P] **2 Rules and regulations**

Underline the correct word(s) in each sentence.
1. You **don't have to/must** save the document before you turn off the computer.
2. In Germany people **must/mustn't** be 18 before they are allowed to drive a car alone.
3. You **mustn't/don't have to** forget to lock the door when you close the shop.
4. A shop assistant **is allowed to/must** serve customers in a shop.

[P] **3 Paraphrasing**

Give definitions of the following words and use relative clauses.

Example: A computer is a machine which stores documents.

1. A shop owner ______________________________
2. An earphone ______________________________
____
3. A shop assistant ______________________________
4. A smoking area ______________________________

Ich kann jetzt ...

1. Kunden auf den richtigen Umgang mit Waren hinweisen. ○○○
2. den Kunden Pflegehinweise zu Produkten geben. ○○○
3. Regeln und Vorschriften, die im Laden Gültigkeit haben, erläutern. ○○○
4. angemessen auf Kundeneinwände reagieren. ○○○
5. verärgerte Kunden beruhigen und ihnen Lösungen für ihre Probleme anbieten. ○○○

☺☺☺ = Kann ich schon!
☺☺ = Kann ich ein bisschen!
☺ = Kann ich bald!

to burn	(ver)brennen	**to lock**	abschließen

Phrases: Special sales situations

Handling goods

You are allowed to touch the goods.	Es ist Ihnen gestattet, die Ware anzufassen.
Please look at the label for more information about the product.	Sehen Sie sich bitte das Etikett an, um mehr Informationen zu erhalten.
I'm sorry, but you mustn't touch the goods.	Es tut mir leid, aber Sie dürfen die Ware nicht berühren.
You can try out the product if you want.	Sie können das Produkt ausprobieren, falls Sie es wünschen.
You must wash these clothes by hand.	Sie müssen diese Kleidung von Hand waschen.
Don't iron this product with low/high heat.	Bügeln Sie dieses Produkt nicht bei niedriger/hoher Hitze.
This material is extremely flammable.	Dieses Material ist sehr leicht entflammbar/brennbar.

Explaining rules and regulations

I must tell you that you are not allowed to buy these products.	Ich muss Ihnen sagen, dass es Ihnen nicht erlaubt ist, diese Produkte zu kaufen.
You mustn't bring food/ice cream/pets into this shop.	Sie dürfen kein Essen/Eis/Haustier mit in diesen Laden nehmen.
You mustn't smoke here.	Sie dürfen hier nicht rauchen.

Dealing with customer complaints

What exactly happened?	Was ist genau passiert?
I can see your point.	Ich kann das nachvollziehen.
That's really annoying, Sir/Madam.	Das ist wirklich ärgerlich.
Let me make you a suggestion.	Lassen Sie mich Ihnen einen Vorschlag unterbreiten.
We can give you a replacement for your product.	Wir können Ihnen für das Produkt Ersatz anbieten.
We accept returns within two weeks after the purchase.	Wir akzeptieren Rückgaben innerhalb von zwei Wochen nach dem Kauf.
The problem is easy to solve.	Das Problem ist leicht zu lösen.
I can show you how it works.	Ich kann Ihnen zeigen, wie es funktioniert.
That can happen sometimes, but ...	Das kann manchmal passieren, aber ...
I can understand what you're saying.	Ich kann nachvollziehen, was Sie sagen.
That can easily be adjusted. Let me show you ...	Das kann leicht eingestellt werden, lassen Sie es mich Ihnen zeigen ...

Convincing upset customers

I will do my best to serve you personally.	Ich werde mein Bestes tun, Sie persönlich zu bedienen.
We are sorry for all the inconvenience caused.	Es tut uns leid, dass wir Ihnen Unannehmlichkeiten bereitet haben.
I can make you an offer.	Ich kann Ihnen ein Angebot machen.
We don't want to lose loyal customers.	Wir möchten keine treuen Kunden verlieren.

After-sales services 8

Am Ende dieser Unit kann ich ...

→ Gründe für eine Rückrufaktion bei Produkten nennen.
→ positive und negative Feedbacks von Kunden verstehen.
→ angemessen auf Kundeneinwände reagieren und ihnen Lösungsvorschläge unterbreiten.
→ Entschuldigungsbriefe an Kunden verfassen.

Online Link
808225-0008

A Product recall

[R/P] **1 Reasons for a recall**

There can be different reasons for a product recall. Look at the photos and match them to possible reasons 1.–4. Write down the right number in the box next to the photo.

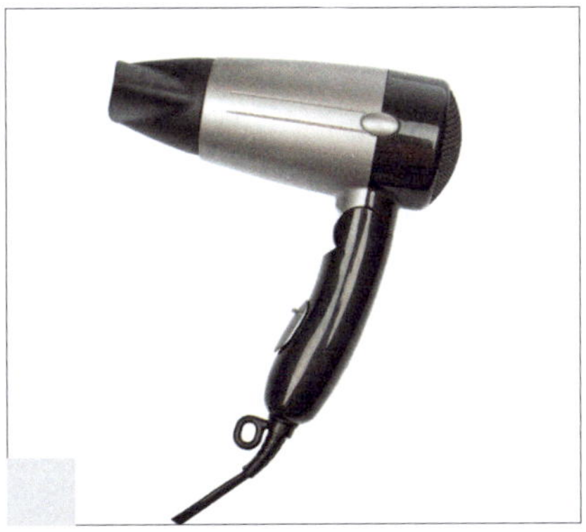

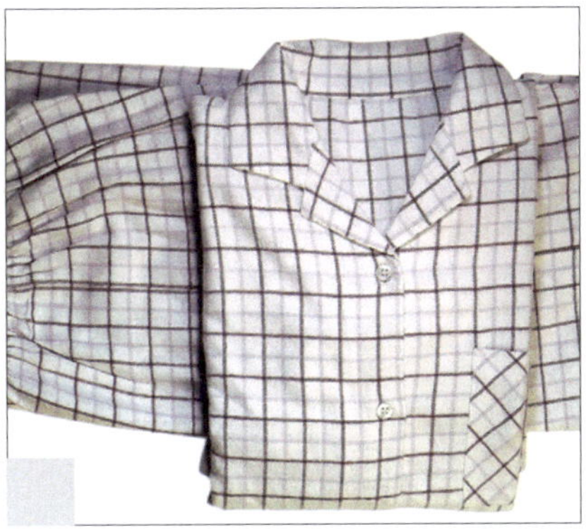

1. It may get too hot and burn your hair.
2. The material can damage your health in the long run.
3. It could easily break down because of a construction fault.
4. If you use it in the sun it will perhaps explode.

[P] **2 Problems with product recalls**

A product recall is the last thing producers want to do. Write down at least two reasons.

to damage the company's reputation • to lose trust in • to unsettle customers

____

____

recall Rückrufaktion
to damage beschädigen
in the long run auf lange Sicht
construction fault Konstruktionsfehler
to explode explodieren
trust Vertrauen
to unsettle beunruhigen

B Dealing with product recalls

[R/P] 1 Reading comprehension

Product recall for bathroom scale, item no 2011
Customer helpline +49-531-202020

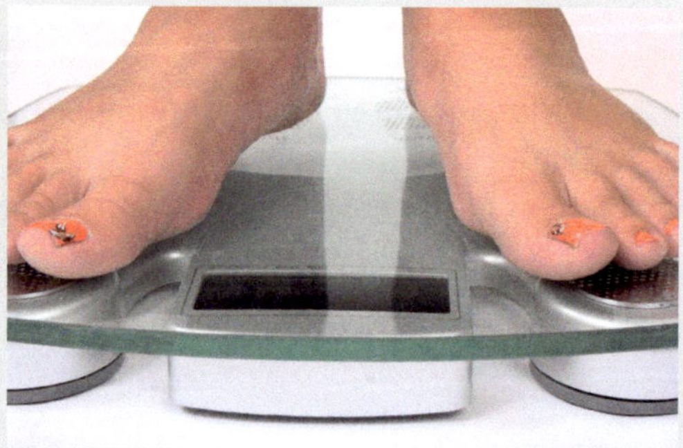

Press release

Dear Users,

We are very sorry to inform you that because of a construction fault, our bathroom scale, item no 2011, shows the wrong weight.

Therefore, we kindly ask all customers who have this item to bring your bathroom scale back to the shop where you bought it. The assistants will give you a full refund or you can have the bathroom scale replaced by a different one.

We apologise for the inconvenience and have asked the shops to give you a voucher for €20 as a compensation. You can spend the voucher in the shop where you bought the product.

We hope for your further trust in our products and will do our best to meet your needs in the future. If you have any questions, please call our 24-hour helpline.

Ulf Martens
Vice president
Bathroom Equipment and More Ltd

Read the text and answer the questions.

1. Why does the producer have to recall the bathroom scales?

   ____

2. What should the customers do?

   ____

3. What does the producer offer for the inconvenience?

   ____

4. What should customers do if they have any further questions?

   ____

[R/P] 2 Vocabulary work

Read the press release again and find the right words for the following explanations.

1. You use it to weigh yourself: ______________________________
2. It is like money and you get goods or services for it: ______________________________
3. The money that you get when you give back a product: ______________________________
4. Another word for hotline: ______________________________

press release Pressemitteilung	**item** Artikel	**to spend** ausgeben
bathroom scale Gewichtswaage	**refund** Rückerstattung	**to meet sb's needs** die Bedürfnisse von jdm. erfüllen
helpline telefonischer Beratungsdienst	**to apologise** sich entschuldigen	
	compensation Schadensersatz	

C Customer feedback

[R/P] **1 Listening: Talking to a friend**
15

Listen to the conversation between Paul, the satisfied customer of a furniture shop, and his friend, Frank. Then complete the sentences.

1. Frank finds Paul's new furniture ______________________________ ______________________________.
2. Paul has bought his furniture at Meyer's for ______________________________ ______________________________.
3. The furniture shop has always offered the best ______________________________.
4. Two years ago Paul wasn't satisfied because ______________________________ ______________________________.
5. But Paul is still a loyal customer because ______________________________ ______________________________.

[R/P/I] **2 Customer suggestions**

Work with a partner and match the sentence parts. Draw lines.

1. If the aisles in the supermarket are wider,
2. If the restaurant offers more meals,
3. If you clean the bathroom,
4. If you accept credit cards,
5. If you open on Sundays,

a) it will be easier to push the trolley past the shelves.
b) I will go shopping together with my whole family.
c) I won't have to count my money at the cash desk.
d) we will have a better choice.
e) I will use it.

[P/I] **3 Role play: Reacting to customer complaints**

Work with a partner. One of you is a shop manager, the other one is a shop assistant. Discuss how you should deal with the following complaints. Then change roles.

Example: Elderly customers need help after they make their purchase.
Assistant: If we help elderly customers after their shopping, we'll need more shop assistants.
Manager: Yes, somebody should take their shopping to the car.

→ See phrases on page 68.

1. A customer has brought back a product with a construction fault and asks for a refund.
2. Many customers want to have a shopping bag for free.
3. Some customers want to take the lift up to the fourth floor but it is often out of order.
4. A customer wants to buy a product that is sold out.

furniture	Möbel	**on time**	pünktlich	**past**	vorbei
to deliver	liefern	**to share**	teilen		

GRAMMAR SPOT ***If*-Sätze (Bedingungssätze) Typ 1**

Ein Bedingungssatz besteht aus einem *if*-Satz und einem Hauptsatz. Der *if*-Satz des Typs 1 beschreibt eine Bedingung und der Hauptsatz drückt aus, was unter bestimmten Bedingungen in der Zukunft geschehen wird oder nicht geschehen wird.
Bildung: *if + simple present* *will + verb*
Beispiel: *If you* ***help*** *your colleague, she* ***will be*** *very happy.*

→ Siehe Grammatikanhang auf S. 97.

D Dealing with complaints and apologising

"I've got your letter in front of me now, sir."

[R/P] 16

1 Listening: Asking for a refund

Listen to the dialogue between a dissatisfied English-speaking customer and the customer service of a department store. Then answer the questions.

1. What did Mr Lindsay buy in the leather goods department?

 ______

 ______

2. Why did he call the customer service?

 ______

 ______

3. What did the customer service offer Mr Lindsay first?

 ______

4. But what did Mr Lindsay want to have?

 ______

5. How did the customer service react?

 ______

[M]

2 Mediation

A colleague wants to know why Mr Lindsay called and how the customer service reacted. Listen to the text again and sum it up in German.

______

______

______

______

______

______

______

customer service	Kundendienst	**suitcase**	Koffer	**to expect**	erwarten
		to rely on	sich verlassen auf		

Role play: Different lives

Work with a partner. Partner A uses the information on this page. Partner B uses the information on the next page.

Partner A

1. You are Frank from Germany and you are talking to a young woman from India. First read the information about Frank. Then answer her questions.

Frank
You are 17 years old and you are working as a trainee shop assistant for a big department store in Berlin. You hope to get a job in a home-entertainment shop after you finish your traineeship. You like your work because it is interesting and you enjoy having contact with customers. From Monday to Friday you start work at 9 or 11 a.m. and finish at 6 or 8 p.m. Every second week you have to work on Saturdays from 9 a.m. to 6 p.m. Your boss and colleagues are very friendly. As a trainee you earn 600 euros per month. You spend most of your money on clothes, CDs, your car and going out at the weekend. You have six weeks' holiday and in your holiday you usually go travelling with your girlfriend. You don't have any money problems because you still live with your parents. You have one older sister.

2. Now ask the young woman from India about her life and fill in the table below.

What's your …?
How old …?
How do you feel about/like …?
Where do you …?
What do you …?
How much do you …?
When …?
How long …?

Name: ______________________________

Age: ______________________________

City: ______________________________

Job: ______________________________

Place of work: ______________________________

Boss: ______________________________

Holidays: ______________________________

Payment: ______________________________

Working hours: ______________________________

____

Spends money on: ______________________________

Family: ______________________________

Future plans: ______________________________

Role play: Different lives

Work with a partner. Partner A uses the information on the previous page. Partner B uses the information on this page.

Partner B

1. You are Sharin from India and you are talking to a young man from Germany. Ask him questions about his life and fill in the table below.

What's your ...?
Where do you ...?
How old ...?
How long ...?
When ...?
How do you feel about/like ...?
What do you ...?
How much do you ...?

Name: ____________________

Age: ____________________

City: ____________________

Job: ____________________

Place of work: ____________________

Boss: ____________________

Holidays: ____________________

Payment: ____________________

Working hours: ____________________

____

Spends money on: ____________________

Family: ____________________

Future plans: ____________________

2. Read the information about Sharin. Then answer Frank's questions.

Sharin

You are 16 and come from New Delhi. You live with your four brothers and two sisters in one room. Your parents are very poor and they don't have enough money to send you to school. Your family needs the money that you earn from your work. You work for a company that produces footballs. You work every day of the week from 6 a.m. until 6 p.m. Sometimes you have to work up to 17 hours a day. Then it is too late to go home and you sleep on the floor in the factory. You earn 2,000 rupees a month, which is about 30 euros. Your boss sometimes hits you when you don't work fast enough. You feel unhappy and you don't like your job. Sometimes you spend a bit of money on sweets. You only have twelve days' holiday a year. You would like to open your own fashion shop in the future.

previous vorherig **to hit** schlagen

Communicative crossword

Find a partner. Then choose the left or the right side – your partner takes the other side. Don't look at your partner's side.

Partner A

You and your partner both have the same crossword, but some of the words are missing. Your partner's side shows the words that you need and your side shows the words that your partner needs. (All these words are from Units 1 to 7.)
Help your partner to finish the crossword. First think of good clues to the words on your own side and write them down. Then take turns to ask each other and tell each other your clues.

What's the clue for 2 down?

How do you call someone who …?

Is the first letter a 'C'?/ Does it start/end with a/an …?

Yes, it is./No, …/Yes, it does./No, …

Is it …?

Do you spell it with a/an …?

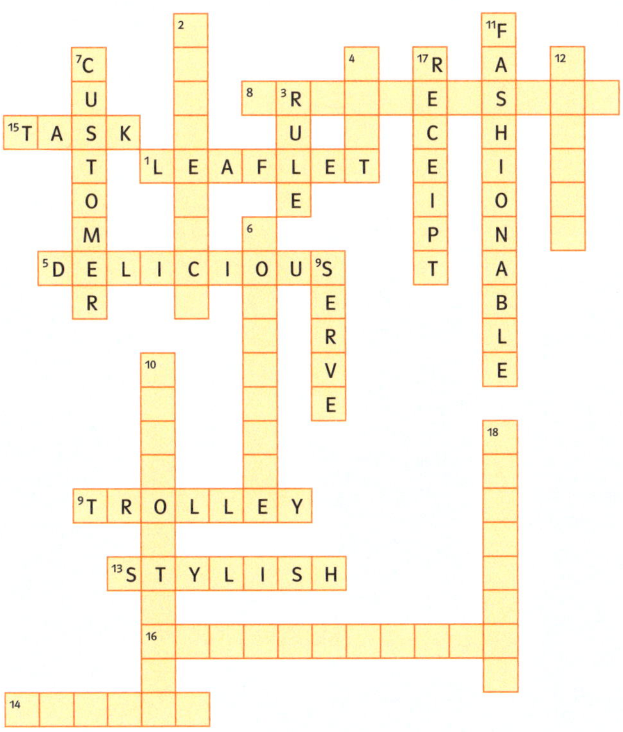

Partner B

You and your partner both have the same crossword, but some of the words are missing. Your partner's side shows the words that you need and your side shows the words that your partner needs. (All these words are from Units 1 to 7.)
Help your partner to finish the crossword. First think of good clues to the words on your own side and write them down. Then take turns to ask each other and tell each other your clues.

What's the clue for 1 across?

How do you call someone who …?

Is the first letter a 'C'?/ Does it start/end with a/an …?

Yes, it is./No, …/Yes, it does./No, …

Is it …?

Do you spell it with a/an …?

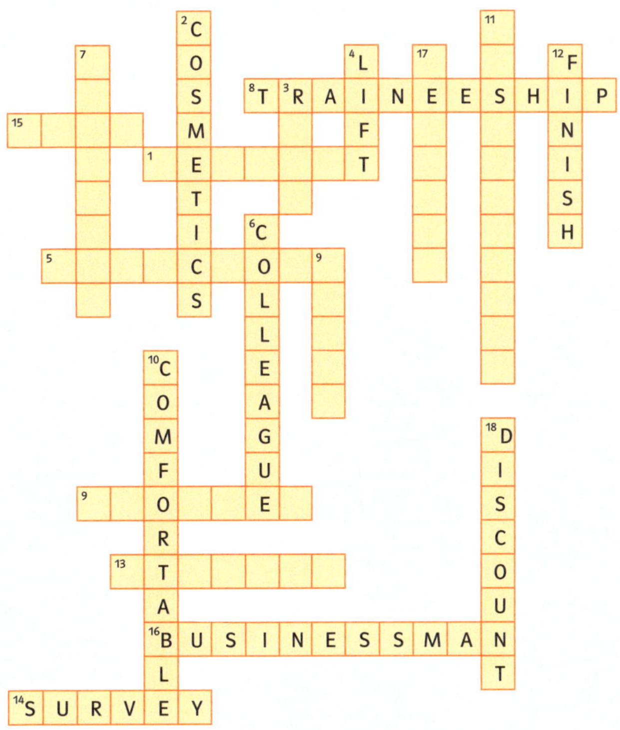

clue Hinweis

Talking about statistics

Find a partner. Then choose side A or B. Don't look at the side that you are not working with.

Partner A

You and your partner have got the same two graphs giving information about mobile phone sales and customer figures of shops in different cities in Britain. However, you each have only one of the two lines that should be on the graphs, so you have to help each other to draw the missing line. First tell your partner what your statistics are about. Then, use the figures at the bottom and the side of the graph and give the information to your partner. (Tip: Draw the line with a pencil first so that you can correct it later if necessary.)

The line starts in the year ... • Between ... and ... sales rise/fall to ... • The percentage rises from ... to ... • There is a gradual/sharp increase/ decrease ... • By ... the percentage is ...

Graph 1: Mobile phone sales to customers aged 18 to 26 in a shop in Liverpool

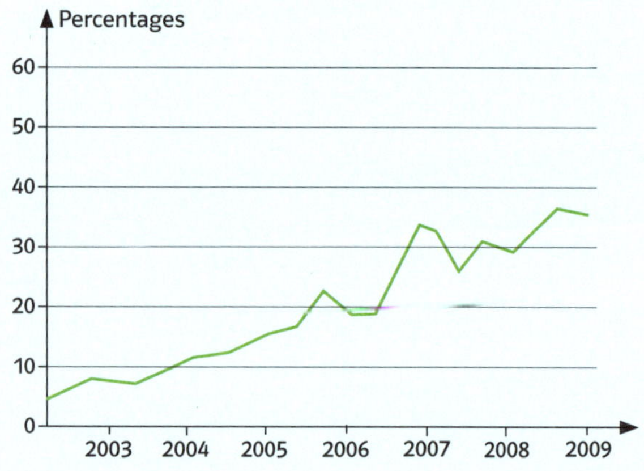

Graph 2: Customer figures of a fashion shop in London

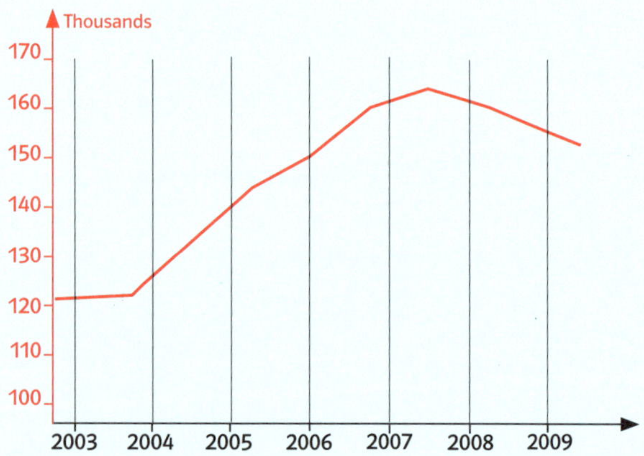

Partner B

You and your partner have got the same two graphs giving information about mobile phone sales and customer figures of shops in different cities in Britain. However, you each have only one of the two lines that should be on the graphs, so you have to help each other to draw the missing line. First tell your partner what your statistics are about. Then, use the figures at the bottom and the side of the graph and give the information to your partner. (Tip: Draw the line with a pencil first so that you can correct it later if necessary.)

The line starts in the year ... • Between ... and ... sales rise/fall to ... • The percentage rises from ... to ... • There is a gradual/sharp increase/ decrease ... • By ... the percentage is ...

Graph 1: Mobile phone sales to customers aged 18 to 26 in a shop in Bristol

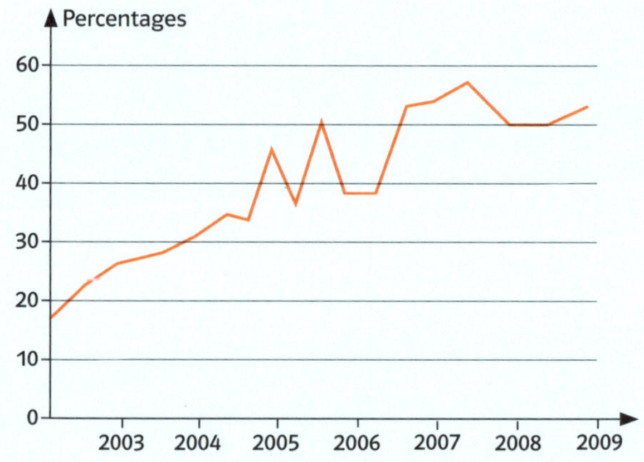

Graph 2: Customer figures of a fashion shop in Manchester

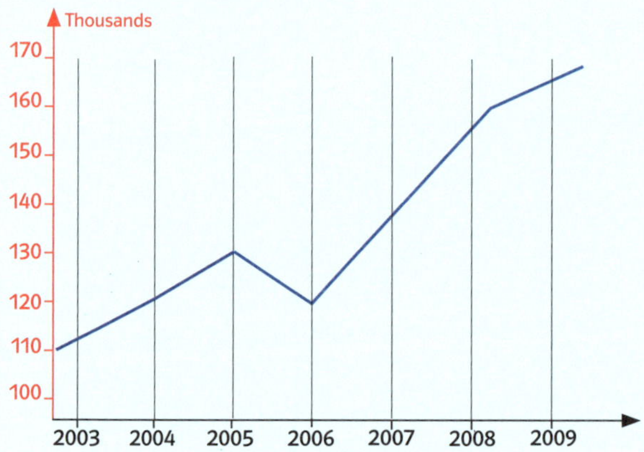

graph	Diagramm	**to rise**	steigen	**sharp**	scharf, stark
figure	Zahl	**gradual**	allmählich		

[R/P] **3 Letter to a customer**

Mr Wienzek has written to Mr Lindsay. Read the letter and then match points 1.–10. to its parts. Write the numbers in the boxes.

1. customer's name and address
2. stating the problem
3. offering compensation
4. the date
5. signature block
6. apologising
7. the company's name and address
8. salutation
9. subject line (what the letter is about)
10. reference line

☐ Schönfelder Warenhäuser
Alexanderplatz 5
39104 Magdeburg

☐ Your ref/Ihr Zeichen: LW05L   Our ref/unser Zeichen: FW/nm

☐ 12 May 2008

☐ Mr Lindsay
Magdeburger Straße 21
39175 Biederitz

☐ Dear Mr Lindsay,

☐ <u>**Your complaint with our customer service**</u>

☐ I have been told that you called our customer service to make a complaint about a suitcase that you had bought in our store. In the meantime our producer has informed us that the wrong locks were used for the suitcases.

☐ We will therefore accept your wish for a refund. As we do not want to lose you as a loyal customer, we also enclose a voucher for € 20.

☐ We apologise for the inconvenience and hope to welcome you again in our stores.

☐ Yours sincerely,
Frank Wienzek
Customer service

[P] **4 Writing a letter**

Write a letter to a customer who complained about the bad quality of a handbag with the customer service two weeks ago. Use your exercise book.

→ See phrases on page 68.

HIER UND DORT Geschäftsbriefe

Wichtige Unterschiede zwischen einem englischen und deutschen Geschäftsbrief sind:

1. Nach der Anrede ist der erste Buchstabe des ersten Satzes ein Großbuchstabe.
   Beispiel: *Dear Sir or Madam, **We** would like ...*
2. Wenn nach der Anrede ein Komma folgt, muss nach der Grußformel ebenfalls eines gesetzt werden. Es kann auch in beiden Fällen entfallen.
   Beispiel: *Dear Sir or Madam ... Yours faithfully/Dear Mr Black, ... Yours sincerely,*
3. *Yours faithfully* bzw. *Yours sincerely* entspricht im Deutschen ‚Mit freundlichen Grüßen'. *Yours faithfully* wird bei einer allgemeinen Anrede, *Yours sincerely* bei einer personenbezogenen Anrede (*Dear Mr .../Mrs ...*) verwendet.
4. Die Betreffzeile (z.B. *Your invoice from ...*) kommt nach der Anrede.
5. Beim Datum wird der Monat ausgeschrieben.

signature Unterschrift	**reference line** Bezugszeichenzeile	**in the meantime** in der Zwischenzeit
salutation Anrede		**to enclose** beilegen
subject line Betreffzeile		

GRAMMAR SPOT ***Present perfect* und *simple past***

Das ***simple past*** wird für vergangene Ereignisse verwendet, die abgeschlossen sind und keinen Bezug mehr zur Gegenwart haben. Häufige Signalwörter sind: *last, yesterday, ago.*
Das ***present perfect*** wird verwendet

1. für Ereignisse, die in der Vergangenheit begonnen haben und die noch nicht abgeschlossen sind bzw. deren Ergebnisse für die Gegenwart noch von Bedeutung sind.
   Häufige Signalwörter sind: *(not) yet, this year/month, never, ever, for, since.*
   since = seit (für Zeitpunkt) *for* = seit (für Zeitraum)
   Beispiel: *I haven't been to school* ***for two days****. I have been at home* ***since Monday****.*
2. für Ereignisse, die gerade abgeschlossen wurden.
   Beispiel: *I have just done my homework.*

→ Siehe Grammatikanhang auf S. 93/94.

[R] **5 Present perfect or simple past?**
Underline the correct verb forms in the following sentences.

1. I **have not been to/was not** in Spain during the past two years.
2. Elvira **bought/has bought** a new washing machine yesterday.
3. I **have started/started** my traineeship at the department store one year ago.
4. René **hasn't seen/didn't see** his boss since Monday.
5. We **had/have had** a new colleague at work for two weeks.

Skills: Interpreting diagrams
Statistics and diagrams often illustrate or explain something. When you compare countable things (for example, people) you should use *more, the most, fewer, the fewest.* When you compare uncountable things (for example, time) you should use *more, the most, less, the least.*

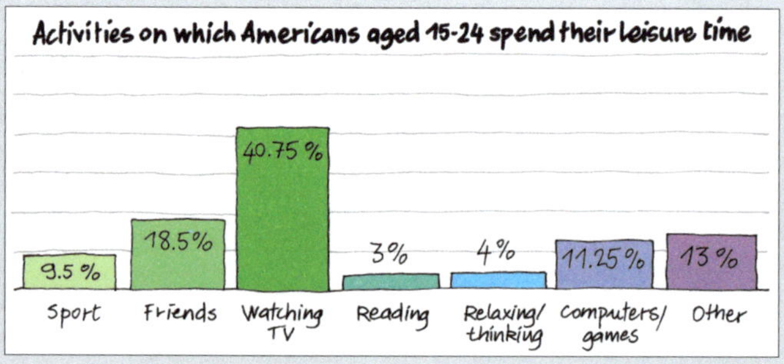

1 Analysing a bar chart
Use the information in the bar chart and answer the questions.

1. What percentage of young Americans spend their leisure time on sport?

____

2. What percentage of their time do they spend on computers and games?

____

2 What is right?
Complete the sentences with *more, the most, less* or *the least.*

Young Americans spend (1) __________ time on sport than with their friends. But they spend (2) ______________ time relaxing or thinking than reading. The activity on which they spend (3) ______________ time is watching TV. The activity on which they spend (4) ________________ time is reading.

to illustrate	veranschaulichen	**leisure time**	Freizeit	**percentage**	Prozentsatz
countable	zählbar	**bar chart**	Balkendiagramm		

E Checking

[R/P] **1 Simple past or present perfect?**
Use the verbs in the box and complete the sentences in the simple past or present prefect.

agree • be • campaign • have • not start • not think • not offer • spend • talk

My boss and I (1) ________________ two weeks in our branch in Eisenach last month. It (2) ____________ really interesting and we (3) ____________ a great time there. For example, they (4) __________________ for fair-trade products for a month now. Our store (5) ____________________ any fair-trade products yet. Why (6) ______________ we ______________ such a campaign last month? I think it's because we (7) ______________ ever ________________ about it. So yesterday I (8) ________________ to my boss and he (9) ____________________ that we will start a campaign next month. I think that's great!

[R/P] **2 'Since' or 'for'?**
Read the sentences and put in *'since'* or *'for'*.

1. I have known my teacher __________ several months.
2. Our shop has been closed __________ Christmas.
3. Karim has been very happy __________ he started his traineeship last year.
4. Ella has been responsible for unpacking the goods __________ six weeks.
5. My friends have had a permanent job __________ they finished their traineeships last year.

[R] **3 False friends**
Cross out the wrong words.
I will **get/become** more money if I work harder. Look, this is a photo **from/of** Mr Wienzek. He always **cooks/makes** coffee for us. Yesterday we even **went/have gone** to the cinema together. I think our **chef/boss** is a really nice person.

[R/P] **4 Reacting in the right way**
Use the sentence parts and form at least six sentences.

If a product is	broken incomplete damaged the wrong size not working properly of bad quality ...	you should	exchange it. repair it. replace it offer a voucher. reduce the price. give a refund. ...

Ich kann jetzt ...

1. Gründe für eine Produktrückrufaktion nennen. ○○○
2. positive und negative Feedbacks von Kunden verstehen. ○○○
3. angemessen auf Kundeneinwände reagieren und Lösungsvorschläge unterbreiten. ○○○
4. Entschuldigungsbriefe an Kunden verfassen. ○○○

☺☺☺ = Kann ich schon!
☺☺ = Kann ich ein bisschen!
☺ = Kann ich bald!

fair trade fairer Handel

Phrases: After-sales talk

Making a product recall

We are sorry to inform you that we have to recall the product because of a construction fault.	Es tut uns leid, Sie darüber informieren zu müssen, dass wir wegen eines Konstruktionsfehlers das Produkt zurückrufen müssen.
We apologise for the inconvenience.	Wir entschuldigen uns für die Umstände/Unannehmlichkeiten, die wir Ihnen bereitet haben.
We hope for your trust in our products.	Wir hoffen auf Ihr Vertrauen in unsere Produkte.
We will do our best to meet your needs in the future.	Wir werden unser Bestes tun, um Ihre Bedürfnisse in Zukunft zu befriedigen.
If you have any more questions, please call our 24-hour hotline.	Sollten Sie in dieser Angelegenheit weitere Fragen haben, rufen Sie bitte unsere 24-Stunden-Hotline an.

Dealing with complaints and apologising

Our shop offers the best service and prices possible.	Unser Geschäft bietet Ihnen den besten Service und die bestmöglichen Preise.
We will give you a refund if you aren't satisfied at all.	Wir werden Ihnen eine Rückzahlung/Kostenerstattung geben, falls Sie überhaupt nicht zufrieden sind.
Thank you for informing us about the problem.	Vielen Dank, dass Sie uns über das Problem in Kenntnis gesetzt haben.
I can see why you are so upset.	Ich kann nachvollziehen, warum Sie so aufgebracht sind.
We have been informed by our producer that it was his fault.	Wir sind von unserem Hersteller informiert worden, dass es sein Fehler war.
We don't want to lose you as a loyal customer.	Wir möchten Sie als loyalen Kunden nicht verlieren.
We enclose a small gift/a voucher as compensation.	Wir legen ein kleines Geschenk/einen Gutschein als Wiedergutmachung bei.

Getting goods delivered 9

Am Ende dieser Unit kann ich ...

→ ein Telefongespräch inhaltlich richtig wiedergeben.
→ die Bestandteile englischer Geschäftsbriefe nennen.
→ Handelskorrespondenz korrekt verfassen und deren Inhalte wiedergeben.
→ Lieferungs- und Zahlungsbedingungen nennen und begründen.

Online Link 808225-0009

A Making an enquiry

[R/P] 17

1 Listening: Calling a potential supplier

Listen to the telephone conversation and sum it up with the help of the photos.

1. ______________________________

2. ______________________________

3. ______________________________

4. ______________________________

enquiry	Anfrage	**to interrupt**	unterbrechen
supplier	Lieferant	**wristwatch**	Armbanduhr

B A business letter

[R/M] **1 Reading comprehension**

Read the enquiry that was sent to British Jewellery. Then use a dictionary and translate the following words and phrases into German.

1. with reference to = ____________________
2. as requested = ____________________
3. to extend the range of products = ____________________
4. trade discounts = ____________________
5. terms of delivery and payment = ____________________
6. to look forward to = ____________________
7. Yours sincerely = ____________________

Schrader Schmuck

Ihre ERSTE Adresse für Schmuck in Düsseldorf und Umgebung

Königsallee 2100, 40200 Düsseldorf, Germany
Telefon: 0211–6034808, Fax: 0211–6034809, E-Mail: schschmuck@aol.de

British Jewellery Ltd
35 Manchester Road
Bristol
AC5 6BA
Great Britain

Our ref: RS/nm

23 March 20..

Dear Mrs Winter,

Enquiry

With reference to our telephone conversation of 22 March 20.. we send you a written enquiry as requested.

We have studied your latest catalogue for wristwatches that was enclosed with the *Jewellery Journal.* We would be interested in offering some of your wristwatches to our customers.

We are a German jewellery shop with three branches in and around Düsseldorf. We have often been asked by our customers to offer wristwatches and therefore want to extend our range of products. We expect to sell watches of high quality in a growing market.

Please be so kind and make us an offer for 50 each of the following watches:
- model 'valuable', order no AFD 2005, price per item: € 350,–
- model 'stylish', order no BAC 2010, price per item: € 400,–
- model 'uncompromising', order no EDF 2009, price per item € 800,–

We would appreciate if you sent us photos of the products for our advertising campaign. Please also inform us about trade discounts and your usual terms of delivery and payment.

Thank you in advance for your reply. We look forward to hearing from you soon.

Yours sincerely,
Nadia Meier
Purchasing assistant

to request	bitten	**to grow**	wachsen	**reply**	Antwort
to expect	erwarten	**in advance**	im Voraus		

[P/I] **2 Paraphrasing**

Choose a part of the letter from the box and explain it to a partner. She/He tries to guess which part you are explaining.
Example: date: In this part of the letter you say when it was written.

customer's name and address • reference line • salutation • signature block • subject line • supplier's name and address

[P/I] **3 The date**

How should you write the dates in a letter? Write them down. Then read them with a partner.

1. 24.03.61: ____________________
2. 07.11.91: ____________________

HIER UND DORT Datum

Die folgenden Schreibweisen für ein Briefdatum sind üblich:
1. in Großbritannien: *5 October 20..* oder *5th October 20..*
2. in den USA: *October 5, 20..* oder *October 5th, 20..*

[R/P] **4 British and American addresses**

Use the information in the boxes and write down the addresses.

1. *CA 95621 • 55 Rubio Street • Los Angeles • USA • Mrs Rosa Johnson*

2. *Eastbourne • Great Britain • 27 Beach Street • Fashion Design • NR2 2 PA*

HIER UND DORT Adressen

Adressen in Großbritannien und den USA haben die folgende Form:

Mr John Black	Mrs Betty Jones
15 Crown Street	121 Santa Barbara Boulevard
Manchester	Portland, OR 87662
WL4 2DA	USA
Great Britain	

[R] **5 Salutation and complimentary close**

Match the salutations to the right complimentary close. Draw lines.

1. Dear Sir or Madam	Yours sincerely,
2. Ladies and Gentlemen:	Sincerely yours
3. Dear Mr Brown,	Yours faithfully
4. Dear Ms Johnson	Yours truly/Very truly yours

[P] **6 Writing an enquiry**

You are working in the toy department of a department store and you need a supplier of high-quality dolls. You saw an advert in *The Guardian*. Write an enquiry and ask for the catalogue, price list, trade discounts and the terms of delivery and payment. Use your exercise book.

→ See phrases on page 76.

complimemtary close Grußformel

HIER UND DORT Anrede und Briefabschluss

Je nachdem, ob der Adressat namentlich genannt wird oder nicht, unterscheiden sich Anrede und Briefabschluss in britischen und amerikanischen Briefen voneinander.

	Anrede	**Briefabschluss**
Firmenbrief: (nicht personenbezogen)	*Dear Sir(s) or Madam(s)* *Dear Ladies and Gentlemen: (AE)*	*Yours faithfully (BE)* *Yours truly/Very truly yours*
Firmenbrief: (personenbezogen)	*Dear Mr Knockwood* *Dear Ms Saunders*	*Yours sincerely (BE)* *Sincerely yours (AE)*

Miss ist als Anrede heutzutage unüblich, stattdessen ist *Mrs* oder *Ms* gebräuchlich.

C Receiving an offer

[R/P] **1 An offer from British Jewellery**

Mrs Winter has sent an offer. Unfortunately, the text is in the wrong order. Put the different parts into the right order and write the numbers in the boxes.

- ☐ Susan Winter
- ☐ Your enquiry of 23 March 20..
- ☐ Dear Ms Meier
- ☐ Encs: 3 photos, terms of delivery and payment
- ☐ Sales department
- ☐ Yours sincerely
- ☐ The total price for all three items (50 each) is €77,500. We are willing to offer you a discount of 10 % off the total price on this order and a further cash discount of 2.5 % for settlement within 15 days of delivery.
- ☐ Thank you for your enquiry about wristwatches. We are pleased to inform you that we have the goods desired in stock (see attached pictures).
- ☐ We are looking forward to receiving your order.
- ☐ Payment should be made according to our terms of delivery and payment, which we enclose with this letter. We will dispatch the goods free of charge by air mail within 4 days after receipt of order.

[R] **2 Simple past or past perfect?**

Underline the right tense.

1. After I **had received/received** your telephone call, I **had sent/sent** you an offer.
2. Mr Green **read/had read** the enquiry which his assistant **had written/wrote**.
3. Before the shop owner **sent/had sent** out the enquiry he **called/had called** the supplier.
4. We **had started/started** selling the product before we **made/had made** a recall.

encs = enclosures Anhang	**to desire** wünschen	**free of charge** kostenlos
further weiter	**in stock** vorrätig	**air mail** Luftpost
cash discount Barzahlungs-rabatt, Skonto	**order** Bestellung	**receipt of order** Auftrags-eingang
settlement Bezahlung	**according to** gemäß	
	to dispatch abschicken	

GRAMMAR SPOT ***Simple past* und *past perfect***

Das ***simple past*** wird für vergangene Ereignisse verwendet, die abgeschlossen sind und keinen Bezug zur Gegenwart haben. Häufige Signalwörter sind *last, yesterday, ago*.
Das ***past perfect*** wird für Ereignisse verwendet, die vor einem bestimmten Zeitpunkt in der Vergangenheit stattgefunden haben, oft in Verbindung mit Wörtern wie *after* oder *before*.
Beispiele: ***Before I went** to school, I **had packed** my schoolbag.*
ABER: ***After I had packed** my schoolbag I **went** to school.*

→ Siehe Grammatikanhang auf S. 93/94.

D Placing an order

[R/I] **1 Business phrases**

Complete the phrases with the verbs from the box. Compare your answers with your partner's.

to dispatch • to enclose • to extend • to grant • to look forward to • to make

1. ____________ an enquiry
2. ____________ goods
3. ____________ trade discounts
4. ____________ photos
5. ____________ the range of products
6. ____________ a reply

[M/P] **2 Writing an order**

Frau Meier will Waren bei British Jewellery bestellen. Verwenden Sie die Informationen auf den Seiten 70 und 72 sowie die Angaben unten und in der Box. Schreiben Sie die Bestellung in Ihr Heft.

We would like to place the following order for ... • We accept ... • The goods should be dispatched ...

- Bedanken Sie sich für das Angebot, die Fotos und die Unterlagen zu den Lieferungs- und Zahlungsbedingungen.
- Bestellen Sie jeweils 50 Armbanduhren der Marken ‚stylish', ‚uncompromising' und ‚valuable' im Gesamtwert von €77 500.
- Sagen Sie, dass Sie mit den Lieferungs- und Zahlungsbedingungen einverstanden sind.
- Teilen Sie mit, dass die Ware nach Auftragseingang sofort verschickt werden soll.
- Sagen Sie, dass Sie sich auf den Erhalt der Ware freuen.
- Schließen Sie den Brief formgerecht ab.

→ See phrases on page 76.

E Delivery and payment

[R/P/M] **1 Confirming an order**

British Jewellery confirms the order. Sum up the e-mail in German. Use your exercise book.

Your order of 4 April 20..

Dear Ms Meier,
Many thanks for your order for wristwatches of 4 April 20..
We are pleased to confirm your order in every detail.
Please note that the goods will be delivered to you on 10 April 20.. by airmail free of charge.
We would kindly like to remind you that we can offer you a further discount of 2.5% for settlement within 15 days of delivery. We would appreciate a payment by credit card or bank transfer. We are certain you will be fully satisfied with our products.
Yours sincerely,
Anoop Nayak
Sales department

to place	*hier:* erteilen	**to confirm**	bestätigen	**bank transfer**	Banküberweisung
to grant	gewähren	**to remind**	erinnern		

[R/P] **2 Paying for goods**

How would you pay for the following goods? Choose the most suitable methods of payment from the box and write them down. Then discuss with a partner why you chose particular methods of payment.
Example: I would pay for a pencil in cash because it doesn't cost a lot.

by bank transfer • by credit card • by EC card • in advance • in cash • in instalments • on receipt of the goods • on receipt of the invoice

1. an ice cream: ____________________
2. a pair of jeans: ____________________
3. a subscription to a magazine: ____________________
4. a product from eBay: ____________________
5. a product from a bookshop in the USA: ____________________
6. a new car: ____________________

[M] **3 Methods of delivery**

Match the German terms 1.–5. with the English terms a)–e). Draw lines.

1. per Luftpost	a) by air freight
2. per Schiff	b) by road
3. per Luftfracht	c) by air mail
4. Straßentransport	d) by train
5 per Zug	e) by ship

Skills: Commercial correspondence

A business letter has to be formal. You have to be polite and should not use short forms (for example, we've) but only the long forms (for example, we have).

1 Practising business language

Replace the crossed out words with phrases from the box and improve the letter.

Ms • on 3 March 20.. • our best • to meet your needs • Please inform us about • some • Thank you very much for your interest. • We look forward to hearing from you. • we will • With reference to • would like • Yours sincerely,

Dear ~~Miss~~ (1) __________ Bricks,

~~Thinking about~~ (2) ____________________ our telephone conversation ~~two days ago~~ (3) ____________________, we ~~want~~ (4) ____________________ to send you ~~lots of~~ (5) ____________________ samples. ~~Let us have~~ (6) ____________________ your special wishes. ~~We'll~~ (7) ____________ do ~~everything we can to make you happy~~ (8) ______________________________. ~~Thanks for the trouble.~~

(9) ______________________________ ~~Hope to hear from you.~~

(10) ______________________________

~~All the best.~~ (11) ____________________

Paul Walters
Sales assistant

in cash	in bar	**on receipt**	bei Erhalt	**subscription**	Abonnement
in instalments	in Raten	**invoice**	Rechnung	**improve**	verbessern

F Checking

[P] 1 Word grid

In the grid there are ten words that you can use for writing an enquiry. Mark the words and write them down.

	A	B	C	D	E	F	G	H	I	J	K	L	M	N	O
1	a	g	t	h	r	e	n	c	l	o	s	e	o	a	y
2	p	u	l	n	e	e	e	a	e	f	c	a	c	p	i
3	f	r	d	a	f	a	r	t	r	c	o	t	o	a	l
4	a	r	u	k	e	c	m	a	r	k	e	t	n	w	q
5	e	r	m	q	r	n	s	l	t	i	s	w	d	y	b
6	m	k	c	d	e	t	m	o	e	n	q	u	i	r	y
7	e	x	t	e	n	d	i	g	r	f	u	n	t	e	s
8	e	x	p	e	c	t	r	u	m	o	o	n	i	t	a
9	o	f	a	k	e	b	d	e	s	r	l	b	o	e	c
10	w	a	s	c	b	g	f	d	e	m	r	a	n	g	e

______________ ______________
______________ ______________
______________ ______________
______________ ______________
______________ ______________

[R/P] 2 Finding the mistakes

There is one mistake in each address. Find it and rewrite the addresses correctly.

1. Mrs Wilson Betty
   London
   WE2 BD4
   12 Malhound Drive

2. Sunshine Fashion
   13 Green Street
   BX5 TA3
   Liverpool

3. Mr John Peak
   131 Delta Avenue
   CA 93332
   San Francisco,

______________ ______________ ______________
______________ ______________ ______________
______________ ______________ ______________
______________ ______________ ______________

[R/P] 3 Simple past or past perfect?

Use the correct tense.

1. After I ____________ **(call)** the company in Cambridge, I ________ **(tell)** my boss about it.
2. Before I ___________ **(place)** the order, I ____________ **(ask)** the supplier to make an offer.
3. I _______________ **(have)** problems with English before I _______________ **(start)** learning with this book.
4. After I _______________ **(help)** Tina to sort the goods, she _____ **(be)** much nicer to me.

Ich kann jetzt …

1. ein Telefongespräch wiedergeben. ○ ○ ○
2. die Bestandteile englischer Geschäftsbriefe nennen. ○ ○ ○
3. englische Geschäftsbriefe korrekt verfassen und deren Inhalte wiedergeben. ○ ○ ○
4. Lieferungs- und Zahlungsbedingungen nennen und diese situationsbezogen begründen. ○ ○ ○

☺☺☺ = Kann ich schon!
☺☺ = Kann ich ein bisschen!
☺ = Kann ich bald!

grid Gitter

Phrases: Business correspondence

Making an enquiry

We can see from your advertisement/ catalogue that ...	Wir können aus Ihrer Anzeige/Ihrem Katalog entnehmen, dass ...
We intend/want to extend our range of products.	Wir beabsichtigen/möchten unsere Produktpalette erweitern.
Please (be so kind and) send us your latest catalogue and price list.	Bitte (seien Sie so freundlich und) übersenden Sie uns Ihren neuesten Katalog mit Preisliste.
Please also inform us about trade discounts and your terms of delivery and payment/ terms and conditions of business.	Bitte informieren Sie uns auch über Handelsnachlässe sowie Ihre Lieferungs- und Zahlungsbedingungen/Geschäftsbedingungen.
We look forward to hearing from you.	Wir freuen uns darauf, von Ihnen zu hören.

Writing an offer

Thank you for your enquiry of ...	Vielen Dank für Ihre Anfrage vom ...
We are pleased to send you the following offer.	Wir freuen uns, Ihnen folgendes Angebot machen/schicken zu können.
We will dispatch the goods immediately after receipt of order.	Wir werden die Waren sofort nach Auftragseingang verschicken.
We are willing to offer you a discount of ... % off the total price of this order.	Wir sind bereit, Ihnen einen Nachlass von ... Prozent auf den Gesamtpreis dieses Auftrags anzubieten.
Additionally we can offer you a cash discount of ... % for settlement within ... days of delivery.	Zusätzlich können wir Ihnen einen Barzahlungsrabatt/Skonto in Höhe von ... Prozent für das Begleichen der Rechnung innerhalb von ... Tagen anbieten.
We would be pleased to receive your order.	Wir würden uns freuen, Ihren Auftrag zu erhalten.

Placing an order

Thank you very much for your offer of ...	Vielen Dank für Ihr Angebot vom ...
We would like to place the following order.	Wir möchten gerne den folgenden Auftrag erteilen.
We agree on/accept your terms and conditions of business.	Wir sind mit Ihren Geschäftsbedingungen einverstanden.
We look forward to receiving your goods.	Wir freuen uns darauf, Ihre Waren zu erhalten.

Delivery and payment

Payment should be made by credit card/ bank transfer/on receipt of the goods/on receipt of the invoice.	Die Bezahlung sollte mit Kreditkarte/ Banküberweisung/bei Erhalt der Ware/bei Erhalt der Rechnung erfolgen.
We also accept payment in advance/in instalments/in cash.	Wir akzeptieren auch Zahlungen im Voraus/ in Raten/in bar.
We will dispatch the goods by air freight/ road/air mail/train/ship.	Wir werden die Ware per Luftfracht/Straßen-transport/Luftpost/Zug/Schiff verschicken.

Job hunting 10

Am Ende dieser Unit kann ich ...

→ über meine und die Jobvorstellungen anderer reden.
→ einen Bewerbungsbrief und meinen Lebenslauf schreiben.
→ mich in einem Vorstellungsgespräch richtig verhalten.

Online Link 808225-0010

A Which job?

[R/P] 18

1 Listening: The right person for the job

Where do these people work? What do you think? Take notes. Then listen to what the people are saying and check your answers. Write down which job each person wanted to do and which job they are doing now.

fashion shop • home-entertainment shop • perfumery • shoe shop • shop for mobile phones • supermarket • tattoo studio

1. Jens: ______________
   job wanted: ______________
   job now: ______________

2. Kristina: ______________
   job wanted: ______________
   job now: ______________

3. Petra: ______________
   job wanted: ______________
   job now: ______________

4. Erkan: ______________
   job wanted: ______________
   job now: ______________

5. Susanne: ______________
   job wanted: ______________
   job now: ______________

[P/I]

2 Your plans

Which job would you like to do after your traineeship? Talk with a partner about your plans.

to hunt *hier:* suchen
to fire entlassen
letter of application Bewerbungsschreiben
career Karriere
to give up aufgeben
job centre Arbeitsamt

B Looking at job adverts

[R/M] **1 Reading comprehension**
Read the information about Marco and the two job adverts.
Then translate the German words and phrases into English.

Hi. My name's Marco. I'm a trainee at Schneider's shoe shop. I've almost finished my traineeship. My marks are fine and I'm very good at English. Next month I'll be a fully qualified shop assistant for shoes. I'd like to stay at Schneider's but they can't employ me. So I'm looking for a new job. Yesterday I saw some job adverts at my vocational school. Perhaps I'll apply for one of them.

For You Shoe Shop
We are looking for a fully qualified
English-speaking shop assistant
to work full-time in our shop. Applicants must have a very good knowledge of English.
The shop currently has five shop assistants and is open from 9 a.m. to 10 p.m. Mo–Fri.
For further information, please contact:
Ms Christiane Gerlich, Tel.: 020 33 60 55

WANTED for Best Prices Shoe Shop:
Part-time assistant for six months
We are looking for a shop assistant for our busy Best Prices shoe shop in the centre of Berlin. Applicants must have at least two years' experience and speak English well. The job is suitable for a person who is looking for a temporary job only.
Please contact: Mr Seebach, Tel.: 0172 346879

1. gesucht = ______
2. Teilzeit = ______
3. Vollzeit = ______
4. wir suchen = ______
5. ist geeignet für = ______
6. voll qualifiziert = ______
7. zur Zeit = ______
8. weitere Informationen = ______
9. mindestens zwei Jahre Berufserfahrung = ______
10. Bewerber/in = ______

[R] **2 Different job offers**
Marco is thinking about the adverts. Match the sentences and draw lines.

1. If I worked at Best Prices,
2. If I worked at For You,
3. If I worked at Best Prices,

a) I would work part-time.
b) I would work there only for six months.
c) the job would be full-time.

[P/I] **3 If I were Marco ...**
If you were Marco, which job would you apply for? Talk to a partner and give reasons.
Start like this: If I were Marco, I would apply for the job at the ... shoe shop because ...

GRAMMAR SPOT ***If*-Sätze (Bedingungssätze) Typ 2** → Siehe Grammatikanhang auf S. 97.

Bedingungssätze des Typs 2 werden benutzt, um über eventuelle Situationen zu sprechen.
Sie werden mit *if + simple past* und *would* gebildet.
Beispiel: *If I **got** the job, I **would be** very happy. / I **would be** very happy if I **got** the job.*

mark	Note	**currently**	zur Zeit
to employ	beschäftigen, einstellen	**temporary job**	befristete Stelle

HIER UND DORT Jobsuche im Ausland

Bei Anzeigen für Stellen im Ausland sollte man auf zusätzliche Angaben achten. So ist es z.B. in den USA nicht üblich, dass der Arbeitgeber die Hälfte der Kosten für die Krankenversicherung oder eine spätere Rentenversicherung bezahlt. Diese Zahlungen kann der Arbeitgeber verweigern oder nach einiger Zeit einfach einstellen. In Stellenanzeigen ist in diesem Zusammenhang z.B. von *medical and/or dental benefits* die Rede.

C Writing a letter of application

[R/P] **1 A letter of application**
Read the advert and complete Francesca's letter of application with words from the box.

apply • as advertised • attended • communication • enjoy • hearing • improved • lessons • position • qualified

Latest Fashion from Milano in Italy currently has a number of positions for shop assistants in Germany to serve our customers at our fashion stores. We need assistants for our Harz region (Bad Harzburg and Goslar) who have an excellent knowledge of English.
For further information, please contact Mr Werner, personnel manager, at ...

Kleeblattweg 27
38527 Meine

Latest Fashion
Königsallee 45
38667 Bad Harzburg

23 June 20..

Dear Mr Werner,

Application for a position as a shop assistant

I am writing to (1) ____________ for the position of shop assistant in your store in Bad Harzburg or Goslar, (2) ____________________ in the *Abendzeitung* of 22 June 20..
As you can see from my enclosed CV, I recently (3) ____________ in retailing and sales as an *Einzelhandelskauffrau*. I did my traineeship at Fashion Meyer, a retailer in fashionable clothing in Meine, and (4) ____________ the Berufsbildende Schulen I in Gifhorn. During this three-year period I attended regular (5) ____________ in English for shop assistants and (6) ____________ my professional (7) ____________________ skills. Last summer I worked for a fashion store in Manchester for four weeks.
The (8) ____________ you offer is just what I am looking for. I (9) ____________ working with people and would also like to have a job where I can use my English.
I would be very happy to be invited for a job interview and look forward to (10) ____________ from you soon.

Yours sincerely,
Francesca Moreno

personnel manager Personalchef
CV (= curriculum vitae) Lebenslauf
to attend besuchen
job interview Bewerbungsgespräch

[P] **2 Writing a letter of application**
Now write your own letter of application to Latest Fashion. Use your exercise book.

D Writing a CV

→ See phrases on page 84.

[P/I] **1 Curriculum vitae**
Read Francesca's CV. Then work with a partner and ask questions about her CV.

When was she born?
What computer programmes ...?
Where did she go to ...?
How well does she speak ...?
What qualifications/work experience did she get at ...?
What does she like doing in ...?
When did she start/finish ...?

CURRICULUM VITAE

Personal details

Name: Francesca Moreno
Address: Kleeblattweg 21
38527 Meine
Tel.: 05304–87401
E-mail: f.moreno@mail.de
Date of birth: 1989

Education and qualifications

Vocational school: 2005–2008 Berufsbildende Schulen I des Landkreises Gifhorn
Qualification: Einzelhandelskauffrau
Secondary school: 1999–2005 Schulzentrum Meine
Qualification: Erweiterter Sek-I Abschluss (Realschule)
Primary school: 1995–1999 Grundschule Am Zellberg, Meine

Work experience

Temporary work: 2008 Job in the production department at VW, Wolfsburg
2008 Job at a fashion store in Manchester

Skills

Computer: Microsoft Word, Microsoft Excel
Languages: German (fluent), Italian (mother tongue), English (good)
Other: Driving licence (since May 2008)

Interests

Travelling, making clothes, singing

[P/I] **2 Writing a CV**
Now write your own CV. Use your exercise book. Then exchange your CV with a partner's and ask each other about your qualifications.

→ See phrases on page 84.

work experience Berufserfahrung	**secondary school** weiterführende Schule	**mother tongue** Muttersprache
education Ausbildung	**primary school** Grundschule	**driving licence** Führerschein

E A job interview

[R/P] 19 **1 Listening: A job interview**

Francesca is having a job interview at Latest Fashion. Listen to the conversation with Mr Werner.

Part 1

First, Mr Winter asks Francesca some questions about her CV. Tick (✓) the correct box.

1. Francesca loves
   - ☐ a) making her own clothes. ☐ b) dancing in the disco. ☐ c) travelling.
2. Francesca sings
   - ☐ a) on TV. ☐ b) in a singing group. ☐ c) at school.

Part 2

They are now talking about the work at Latest Fashion. Complete the following sentence.

Francesca thinks she would be a good shop assistant because she ____________________

____

Part 3

Listen to the end of the interview. Decide whether the statements are true or false.

1. If Francesca got the job she would have to wear clothes from the store. __________
2. Mr Werner will contact Francesca tomorrow about the job. __________

[P/I] **2 Role play: At a job interview**

Work in groups and do role plays of a job interview in English. Use the questions below and your own ideas.

→ See phrases on page 84.

Personnel manager

- What are your hobbies?
- Have you had a job before?
- Where did you go to ...?
- How long have you learned ...?
- What are your favourite subjects?
- Why do you think you would fit in our shop?
- We'll contact you ...

Applicant

- If I got the job, would I have to ...?
- How much will I earn if I get the job?
- When can I expect to receive an answer from you?

[P] **3 At a job interview**

Describe the cartoon in about 50 words. Who is there, where are they and what is happening? What might the interviewer say to the applicant? Will the applicant get the job? Write in your exercise book.

subject Fach

[R/P] **4 Using the passive**

Make passive sentences. Use the simple present or the simple past.

Example: Yesterday we were asked (ask) by our customers to make an offer for wristwatches.

1. Once a week the products __________ **(deliver)** by air mail. 2. Your goods __________ **(damage)** in an accident last week. 3. The bathroom scale __________ **(replace)** last Friday. 4. Usually the refunds __________ **(send)** by our customer service office. 5. The best prices __________ **(offer)** to loyal customers only.

GRAMMAR SPOT Das Passiv

Passivsätze werden mit *to be* und dem Partizip Perfekt (3. Form) gebildet. Die verschiedenen Zeiten werden mit den entsprechenden Formen von *to be* gebildet:
The product ***is made*** *in Britain. (simple present)*
My wallet ***was produced*** *in China. (simple past)*
Um zu sagen, von wem etwas gemacht wird/wurde, verwendet man im Passiv das Wort *by*:
This letter of application was written ***by*** *Francesca.*

→ Siehe Grammatikanhang auf S. 98.

Skills: Applying for a job

When you apply for a job make sure that you include all information in your letter and CV. Before you send them off, check them carefully and perhaps ask someone else to read them through. Be polite and use long forms (for example, ‚I have' instead of 'I've'). Say why you are the right person for the job and why you are interested in working for them.

1 Tips for job interviews

Copy the table below into your exercise book. Then read the tips for a successful job interview. Write the dos and don'ts into your table.

Dos	Don'ts
1. Find out about the company.	1. Don't go to bed late.
2. ...	2. ...

Before the interview ...
- Find out more about the company. Look on the internet and in newspapers.
- Find out where the company is and plan your journey to the interview.
- Think: what questions will they perhaps ask me and what will I say?
- Go to bed early and sleep.

At the interview ...
- Don't be late! Things can always go wrong with buses, etc.
- Wear nice, clean clothes.
- Smile, be positive and friendly.
- Sit upright – you aren't at home on the sofa.
- Look for eye contact with the interviewer when you talk to him/her.
- Answer the questions but don't talk too much. Don't give very long answers.
- Speak clearly.
- Tell the truth, don't lie.
- When you don't understand a question, say so.
- Ask one or two questions yourself at the end of the interview to show interest.
- Thank the interviewer, smile again and leave the room quietly.

journey	Reise	**truth**	Wahrheit
upright	aufrecht	**to lie**	lügen

F Checking

[P] 1 If I …
Use the information in the photos and write a sentence about each picture.

1

2

3

4

1. If I saw this building, I would be in ______
2. ______
3. ______
4. ______

[P] 2 The passive
Rewrite the sentences in the passive.
Example: A customer studied your catalogue. → Your catalogue was studied by a customer.

1. We appreciate payment in cash. ______
2. He sent two students to Britain. ______
3. Clive Smith reads the news on the BBC. ______
4. The owner offered Tom a job. ______

[R/M] 3 Finding and translating words
Find the words and phrases from Unit 10. Write them down and translate them into German.

primaryschoolcurriculumvitaetraineeshipqualificationsfullyqualifiedwantedparttimefurtherin
formationknowledgeofEnglishexperiencefulltimecurrentlysecondaryschooltoapplyforajob

______
______
______
______
______
______

Ich kann jetzt …

1. über Jobvorstellungen reden. ○○○
2. über Stellenanzeigen und Bewerbungen sprechen. ○○○
3. mich auf eine Stelle mit einem Bewerbungsbrief und Lebenslauf bewerben. ○○○
4. mich in einem Vorstellungsgespräch richtig verhalten. ○○○
5. sagen was passieren würde, wenn … ○○○

☺☺☺ = Kann ich schon!
☺☺ = Kann ich ein bisschen!
☺ = Kann ich bald!

Phrases: Job application

Job adverts

We are currently looking for a fully qualified shop assistant.	Wir suchen momentan nach einer/einem voll ausgebildeten Verkäuferin/Verkäufer.
We can offer you a full-time/part-time job.	Wir können Ihnen einen Vollzeit-/ Teilzeitarbeitsplatz anbieten.
It's a permanent/temporary job.	Es ist eine dauerhafte/befristete Stelle.
Applicants must have a good/an excellent knowledge of English.	Bewerber müssen über gute/hervorragende Englischkenntnisse verfügen.
The job is suitable for ...	Der Job ist geeignet für ...
You should have at least two years' experience.	Sie sollten über mindestens zwei Jahre Berufserfahrung verfügen.
Please send your application to ...	Bitte schicken Sie Ihre Bewerbung an ...
For further information, please contact ...	Für weitere Informationen setzen Sie sich bitte mit ... in Verbindung.
Our opening hours are from ... to ...	Unsere Öffnungszeiten sind von ... bis ...

Writing a letter of application

I would like to apply for the position of ...	Ich möchte mich auf die Stelle als ... bewerben.
... as advertised in ...	... wie ausgeschrieben/inseriert in ...
I have qualified in retailing and sales.	Ich habe mich für Einzelhandel und Verkauf qualifiziert.
I have improved my professional communication skills.	Ich habe meine kommunikativen Fähigkeiten verbessert.
I enjoy working with people.	Es macht mir Spaß, mit Leuten zu arbeiten.

Writing a CV

primary school/secondary school/vocational school/work experience/skills/interests	Grundschule/weiterführende Schule/ Berufsschule/Arbeitserfahrung/Fähigkeiten

At a job interview

I would like this job because ...	Ich möchte gerne diesen Job machen, weil ...
From your homepage on the internet I've learned that you ...	Auf Ihrer Homepage im Internet habe ich erfahren, dass Sie ...
My hobbies are ...	Meine Hobbies sind ...
When can I expect to receive an answer from you?	Wann kann ich von Ihnen eine Antwort erwarten?

KMK-Musterprüfung (Eurolevel B1, KMK-Stufe II)

Schriftliche Prüfung

Zeit: 90 Minuten
Hilfsmittel: Allgemeines zweisprachiges Wörterbuch
Maximale Punktzahl: 100 Punkte

Online Link 808225-0011

Im Folgenden werden Ihnen vier Aufgaben zur Bearbeitung vorgelegt. Die ersten beiden Aufgaben beziehen sich auf Ihre Fähigkeit, englische Texte (sowohl gesprochene als auch geschriebene) zu verstehen (= Rezeption). Bei der dritten Aufgabe wird von Ihnen erwartet, dass Sie englische Angaben ins Deutsche übertragen (= Mediation). Die vierte Aufgabe verlangt das Schreiben eines englischen Textes (= Produktion).
Die Prüfung beginnt mit der Hörverständnisaufgabe. Alle weiteren Aufgaben können in beliebiger Reihenfolge bearbeitet werden.

Situation
Sie sind Tina Heft, Assistentin der Einkaufsleitung der Modekette MODEWELT in Hamburg. Ihre Chefin, Frau Schmidt, ist durch eine Anzeige in einer Modezeitschrift auf den englischen Strickwarenhersteller Coolwool aufmerksam geworden. Da Sie über ausgezeichnete Englischkenntnisse verfügen, sind Sie aufgefordert, schriftlich und mündlich in Englisch zu kommunizieren.

Rezeption

20 **Aufgabe 1: Hörverständnis** ca. 20 Min. 25 P.

Tina Heft ruft bei Coolwool in England an. Hören Sie aufmerksam zu und notieren Sie Kurzantworten in **deutscher Sprache**, entsprechend den im Memo (s. unten) gemachten Angaben. Berücksichtigen Sie dabei insbesondere die von Coolwool angebotene Produktpalette, die Qualitäten/Größen und die Garantie- und Liefermodalitäten.
Schreiben Sie zuerst die Angaben zum Memo in Ihr Heft.
Dann hören Sie den Dialog zweimal. Notieren Sie Ihre Antworten ins Heft.

MEMO

Für: ____________________ Von: ____________________

Gesprächspartner/in: ____________________ Firma: ____________________

Anruf vom (Datum): ____________________ Uhrzeit: ____________________

Betrifft: ____________________

____

____

____

Aufgabe 2: Leseverständnis ca. 20 Min. 20 P.

Sie sind soeben von einem Woolmark Kongress in London zurückgekehrt. Frau Schmidt hat Sie gebeten, die Zahlen und Fakten über die Preisentwicklung auf dem Wollmarkt zu präsentieren. Dabei dient der Text rechts als Grundlage, um die Entwicklung von 2001 bis 2010 in einer Grafik darzustellen.
Verwenden Sie bitte die Tabelle unten für Ihre Eintragungen.

The international price for wool went up gradually from 650 cents per kg clean wool in 2001 to 760 cents/kg in the middle of 2002. One year later the price dropped to 450 cents/kg. In the following two years the price recovered and reached a maximum of 930 cents/kg at the end of 2005. Unfortunately, until the first quarter of the following year the price fell sharply to a low of 590 cents/kg. Then it picked up again in early 2008 to 810 cents/kg. At the beginning of 2009 it decreased by 40 %. Since then it has picked up again and by the end of 2010 it is expected that the price will rise to 710 cents/kg.

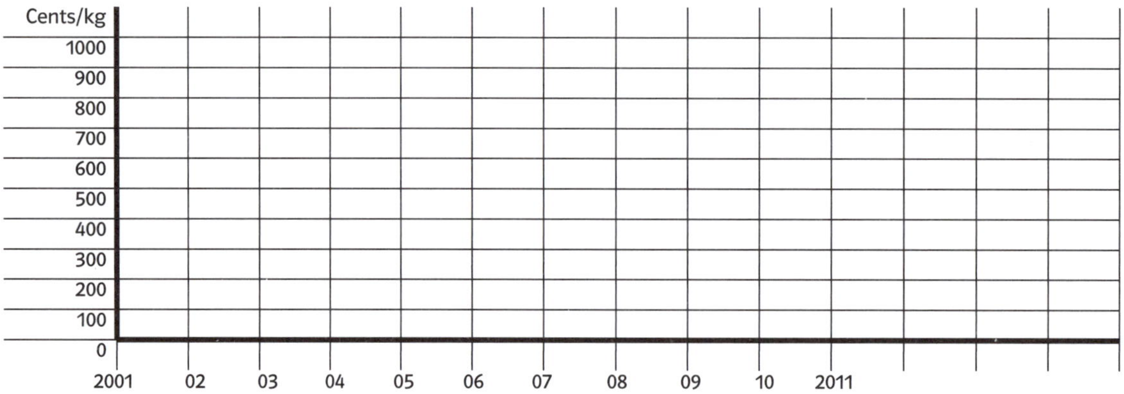

Mediation

Aufgabe 3: Übertragen eines englischen Textes ins Deutsche ca. 25 Min. 30 P.

Ihre Chefin hat in einer internationalen Fachzeitschrift eine Anzeige der Gerarno Ltd, eines Großhändlers für Modebekleidung, gelesen. Frau Schmidt beauftragt Sie, die Anzeige ins Deutsche zu übertragen.
Schreiben Sie Ihren deutschen Text in Ihr Heft.

... GERARNO Ltd
originated as a wholesale business

Expansion continues in the UK and internationally with an emphasis on:

- the analysis of British and international markets to ensure the finest presentation of the products.
- preservation of brand integrity.
- development of the brand image and profile through visual merchandising.

As a result of successful placement in the UK's most greatly respected department stores the brand has a steadily increasing presence.
Our production centre in Hong Kong was established in 1978. The office has a very experienced team of people dedicated to finding new materials and techniques to improve the design aspect of the brand.

We specialise in advanced knitting and machine technology. Different quality garments are manufactured in Hong Kong and shipped to the UK and overseas. The emphasis is on quality, and all staff regularly attend courses to further their knowledge of the garment business.

Features of our ideal GERARNO customer:

- age group 28–55+ years
- classy
- money to invest

Nothing is more important than satisfied customers because:

- satisfied customers are repeat business.
- satisfied customers talk to and influence others.

Produktion

Aufgabe 4: Verfassen eines Faxschreibens ca. 25 Min. 25 P.

Nach einer Woche liegen die gewünschten Unterlagen (Produktpalette, Qualitäten/Größen, Garantie- und Lieferbedingungen) der englischen Firma vor.
Formulieren Sie nun ein Fax in englischer Sprache an den potentiellen Geschäftspartner Coolwool, 47 Brooklands Avenue, Great Wyrley, Walsall WS6 6LF, West Midlands, England, Tel.: 0044-(0)1542-774290, Fax: 0044-(0)1542-774291.
Berücksichtigen Sie neben korrekter Anrede und Grußformel die folgenden Aspekte:

- Bedanken Sie sich höflich für die ausführlichen Informationen.
- Unterstreichen Sie, dass Ihre Kunden eine hochwertige Qualität der Produkte erwarten.
- Betonen Sie, dass Sie hauptsächlich Strickjacken und Röcke für Damen in den Größen L bis XXL benötigen.
- Bitten Sie um einen Probeauftrag über je 500 Stück.
- Teilen Sie der Firma mit, dass Sie von regelmäßigen Lieferungen ausgehen, wenn die Probeartikel Ihren Erwartungen entsprechen.
- Bitten Sie um ein Preisangebot mit Angabe der Lieferungs- und Zahlungsbedingungen und sämtlicher Nachlässe über je 500 Stück.
- Gehen Sie darauf ein, dass Sie im Falle eines Vertragsabschlusses das Angebot des Transportes durch den englischen Hersteller annehmen.
- Schließen Sie Ihr Schreiben freundlich.

Schreiben Sie die Faxvorlage (s. unten) und den englischen Text in Ihr Heft.

Modewelt Exklusive Bekleidung

Hafenstr. 27
23054 Hamburg
Tel.: (040) 242424-0
Fax: (040) 242424-12

TELEFAX

Empfänger/Recipient: ______________________

Datum/Date: ______________________

Seiten/Pages: ______________________

Von/From: ______________________

Betrifft/Subject: ______________________

____

____

Mündliche Prüfung

Zeit: 15 Minuten (plus 20 Minuten Vorbereitungzeit)
Hilfsmittel: Allgemeines zweisprachiges Wörterbuch
Maximale Punktzahl: 30 Punkte

Die mündliche Prüfung ist eine Partnerprüfung und sie besteht aus zwei Teilen. Im ersten Teil werden Sie gebeten, sich zu persönlichen oder beruflichen Themen zu äußern. Im zweiten Teil sollen Sie in Partnerarbeit ein Rollenspiel durchführen. Dazu erhalten Sie Rollenkarten auf denen eine Situation beschrieben ist, die Sie ausspielen sollen. Dabei wird von Ihnen erwartet, dass Sie mit der vorgegebenen Situation sprachlich angemessen umgehen.

Rollenkarte A

Sie sind Angestellte/r der Filiale der britischen Autovermietungsgesellschaft Travis United in Falmouth, Cornwall. Es ist 10:00 Uhr. Das Telefon klingelt und Sie bereiten sich auf eine übliche Anfrage bezüglich der Anmietung eines Fahrzeuges vor.

1. Nennen Sie Ihren Firmennamen und Ihren eigenen Namen und fragen Sie höflich, was Ihr Telefonpartner wünscht.
3. Fragen Sie den Kunden, ob er einen besonderen Fahrzeugwunsch hat.
5. Fragen Sie, für wie lange das Fahrzeug gemietet werden soll.
7. Erklären Sie, dass das Fahrzeug £ 55 pro Tag kostet, inklusive VAT und Vollkasko-versicherung. Es gibt keine Meilenbegrenzung.
9. Sagen Sie, dass es kein Problem ist, das Fahrzeug zum Hotel zu bringen, da die Miete den Transport zu einem vereinbarten Treffpunkt beinhaltet. Bitten Sie Ihren Gesprächspartner um den Namen, die momentane Adresse und die Telefonnummer.
11. Fragen Sie, ob das Alter des Kunden zwischen 21 und 70 liegt und die Führerscheindauer mindestens zwei Jahre beträgt.
13. Bitten Sie um die Nummer und das Ablaufdatum der Kreditkarte.
15. Sichern Sie zu, dass das Auto in der nächsten halben Stunde zum Hotel gebracht wird und der Fahrer die Dokumente zum Unterschreiben mitbringt.
17. Bedanken Sie sich für den Anruf und wünschen Sie dem Anrufer einen angenehmen und sicheren Aufenthalt in Großbritannien.

Rollenkarte B

Sie sind geschäftlich für eine Woche in Großbritannien unterwegs. In Falmouth, Cornwall, gehen Sie zu Ihrem vorgebuchten Hotel und erhalten dort die Telefonnummer der Autovermietungsgesellschaft Travis United, die Sie nun anrufen. Es ist 10:00 Uhr.

2. Eröffnen Sie das Telefongespräch und erklären Sie, dass Sie eine viertürige Limousine mieten möchten.
4. Sagen Sie, dass Sie ein deutsches Fahrzeug bevorzugen.
6. Sagen Sie, dass Sie das Auto für vier Tage benötigen.
8. Geben Sie Ihr Einverständnis zu den unterbreiteten Kosten. Bitten Sie darum, Ihnen das Fahrzeug nun zum Hotel zu bringen.
10. Geben Sie Ihren Namen und Ihre momentane Adresse an: Sea View Hotel, Nelson Street Nr. 15, Tel.: 01326-250544.
12. Bejahen Sie die Frage und sagen Sie, dass Sie 28 Jahre alt sind und Ihren Führerschein seit zehn Jahren haben.
14. Ihre Kreditkartennummer lautet: 5232 2436 2007 und die Karte ist bis Juni 2020 gültig.
16. Danken Sie freundlich für die Mühe und beenden Sie angemessen das Telefongespräch.

10 Tipps zum Englischlernen

TIPP 1
GRAMMATIK

Kaum jemand paukt gerne Grammatik, doch führt kein Weg daran vorbei. Die unregelmäßigen Verben sind dabei die halbe Miete. Wenn Sie die „draufhaben", fallen Ihnen die Zeiten sowie Aktiv/Passiv und *if*-Sätze viel leichter. Nehmen Sie sich jeden Tag ein Verb vor. Überlegen Sie auch, wie sich Verben in Gruppen zusammenfassen lassen (z. B. *drink–drank–drunk* und *sing–sang–sung*).

Und wie wäre es, wenn Sie sich einmal die Woche hinsetzen und vier (beliebige) Sätze aus der aktuellen Unit abschreiben? Auch so prägt sich Grammatik ein!

TIPP 2
PROJEKTARBEIT: GEZIELTE GRUPPENARBEIT

Erfolgreiche Projekt- und Gruppenarbeit braucht Regeln:

- Legen Sie exakt fest, was Sie erarbeiten möchten. Fassen Sie das Thema nicht zu weit, sonst verlieren Sie leicht den Überblick.
- Als Nächstes: Planen Sie die einzelnen Arbeitsschritte. Das ist besonders wichtig, wenn Sie in einer Gruppe arbeiten. Wo finden Sie die notwendigen Informationen? Wer macht was bis wann?
- In welcher Form präsentieren Sie Ihre Ergebnisse? Referat? Plakat? Website? Klären Sie solche Fragen frühzeitig, um dann gezielt und effektiv arbeiten zu können.

TIPP 3
UMGANG MIT LESE- UND HÖRTEXTEN

Lassen Sie sich von längeren Lese- und Hörtexten nicht verrückt machen. Und greifen Sie nicht gleich zum Wörterbuch. Beachten Sie stattdessen folgende Tipps:

- Vor dem ersten Lesen/Hören: Was verraten Überschriften und Bilder über den Inhalt des Textes? Mutmaßen Sie, worum es geht, das hilft beim anschließenden Verstehen.
- Lesen oder hören Sie den Text als Nächstes ein- oder zweimal, ohne an einzelnen Wörtern hängen zu bleiben. Es ist völlig normal, wenn Sie nicht gleich alles verstehen.
- Danach erst ist Detailverständnis gefragt. Bevor Sie das Wörterbuch zücken, überlegen Sie, ob Sie einzelne Wörter, Ausdrücke, ganze Sätze nicht doch aus dem Zusammenhang verstehen können. Dies ist eine ganz eigene Fähigkeit, aber wie alle anderen auch kann sie trainiert werden!

TIPP 4
VOKABELLERNEN

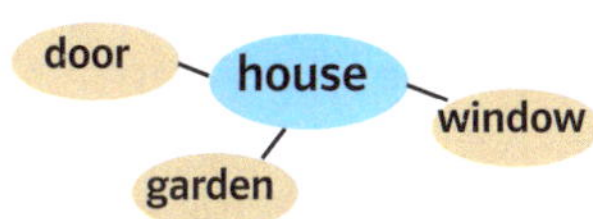

- Lernen Sie regelmäßig Vokabeln, nicht erst am Ende der Unit oder kurz vor der Arbeit. Fünf Vokabeln jeden Tag bringen mehr als eine lange Liste auf einmal.
- Und noch etwas: Stellen Sie Wörter zu Wortfeldern zusammen, z.B. alle Wörter zum Thema *house* oder alle zum Wortfeld *work*. Unser Gehirn lernt und erinnert sich leichter, wenn das Gelernte in Gruppen abgespeichert wird.
- Lernen Sie Vokabeln im Zusammenhang, d.h. in einem kurzen Satz oder einer Wendung. Dann müssen Sie später nicht erst überlegen, wie das Wort verwendet wird. Beispiel: *home – at home – to go home*. Weitere Beispiele finden Sie im Vokabelanhang.

TIPP 5

SPRECHEN UND SCHREIBEN

K
I
S
S

Wetten, Sie finden Lesen und Hören auf Englisch einfacher als Sprechen und Schreiben? Das geht den meisten Leuten so. Der Schlüssel zum Erfolg: *KISS* = ***K**eep **I**t **S**hort and **S**imple*.

Vermeiden Sie lange und komplizierte Sätze, die Sie Wort für Wort ins Englische übersetzen. Konzentrieren Sie sich stattdessen auf einfache, knappe Sätze, bei denen Sie sich sicher fühlen. Lieber einfach und richtig als kompliziert und falsch.

TIPP 6

WÖRTERBUCHARBEIT

Ein zweisprachiges Wörterbuch ist wichtig, hat aber seine Tücken! Denn meistens bietet es mehrere Übersetzungen, und woran erkennt man die richtige? Am besten: Schlagen Sie die Übersetzung, für die Sie sich entschieden haben, als Gegenbeweis in der anderen Hälfte des Wörterbuchs nach.

TIPP 7

KLASSENARBEITEN UND PRÜFUNGEN

- Fangen Sie rechtzeitig mit dem Lernen an, aber hören Sie auch rechtzeitig wieder auf. Nicht bis unmittelbar vor der Arbeit lernen!
- Während der Arbeit: Lesen Sie die Aufgabenstellung genau durch. Sie verschenken unnötig Punkte, wenn Sie nicht auf das antworten, was gefragt ist.
- Auch wenn's nervt: Lesen Sie die Arbeit mindestens einmal durch, bevor Sie diese abgeben. Irgendetwas findet man immer!

TIPP 8

WIE HÄLT MAN EIN REFERAT?

- Das A und O eines guten Referats: Sagen Sie Ihrem Publikum, worüber Sie sprechen werden *(Today I'd like to talk about ...)*, sprechen Sie dann darüber und fassen Sie anschließend zusammen, was Sie gerade gesagt haben!
- Setzen Sie visuelle Hilfen ein. Denn: Wir lernen zu 80 % über das Sehen, nur zu 20 % über das Hören. Schreiben Sie Stichwörter an die Tafel, bereiten Sie eine Folie mit Bildern/Grafiken vor. Davon profitieren nicht nur Ihre Zuhörer, sondern auch Sie – denn so prägt sich der Ablauf Ihres Referats besser bei Ihnen ein.

TIPP 9

MEIN HOBBY? ENGLISCH.

website **pop song** **computer** **hamburger** **jeans**

Englisch begegnet man heute überall – auf Kinoplakaten, in Zeitschriften, im Internet, in der Werbung, im Fernsehen, in Popsongs. Sperren Sie Augen und Ohren auf. Versuchen Sie z.B. Ihr aktuelles Lieblingslied zu verstehen oder schalten Sie, wenn Sie einen Film auf DVD schauen, auf die englische Spur um.

TIPP 10

UND ZUM SCHLUSS ...

Ein kluger Kopf hat einmal gesagt, mit dem Sprachenlernen sei es wie mit dem Autofahren: Übung macht den Meister! Wir können die Theorie noch so gut beherrschen, es ist erst die Praxis, die uns zu guten Autofahrern macht. Auch eine Sprache müssen Sie üben und üben, bis es irgendwann wie von selbst geht und Sie kaum noch Fehler machen. Und denken Sie daran: So schwer ist das alles nicht – das haben schon andere vor Ihnen geschafft!

Grammatikanhang

1 Das *simple present*

A Allgemein

Das *simple present* wird verwendet:
- für Aussagen, die längere Zeit gültig sind.
- um auszudrücken, was jemand regelmäßig tut.

B Mit *sometimes, often*, usw.

Da man mit dem *simple present* ausdrückt, was man regelmäßig tut, wird es oft mit Wörtern wie *usually, normally, sometimes, often, always, never* verwendet. Diese Wörter (Adverbien) stehen immer:
- **vor** einem Vollverb.
- **nach** *to be*.

*I **usually** get up at 7 a.m.*

*I **often** watch TV in the evenings.*

*I'm **always** happy on Fridays.*

C Bildung: Aussagen

Das *simple present* wird aus der Grundform des Verbs (Infinitiv ohne *to*) gebildet. Nach *he/she/it* endet das Verb immer auf -*s* oder -*es*!
1. An die meisten Verben wird einfach -*s* angehängt.
2. Die Endung -*es* wird bei Verben benutzt, die auf *s, ss, x, ch* oder *sh* enden (z. B. *to finish*), da es schwer wäre, nur ein -*s* auszusprechen.
3. Auch die Verben *go* und *do* enden mit -*es*.
4. Ein Sonderfall sind Verben, die auf -*y* enden: *to tidy* → *he tid**ies***.

1. to work	2. to finish
I work he/she/it work**s** we work you work they work	I finish he/she/it finish**es** we finish you finish they finish

3. to go	4. to tidy
I go he/she/it go**es** we go you go they go	I tidy he/she/it tid**ies** we tidy you tidy they tidy

D Bildung: Fragen und Verneinungen
- Fragen im *simple present* werden mit *do* (bei *he/she/it*: *does*) gebildet.
- Verneinungen bildet man mit *don't* (nach *he/she/it*: *doesn't*).

Vorsicht!

Nach *does/doesn't* kommt immer die Grundform des Verbs:

Does he work? (! Does he ~~works~~?)

She doesn't work. (! She doesn't ~~works~~.)

Fragen	Verneinungen
Do I work? Does he/she/it wor**k**? Do we work? Do you work? Do they work?	I don't work he/she/it doesn't wor**k** we don't work you don't work they don't work

2 Das *present continuous*

A Allgemein
Das *present continuous* benutzt man für Aktivitäten, die gerade im Augenblick des Sprechens stattfinden. Oder auch um ein Bild zu beschreiben. Es wird häufig mit Zeitangaben wie *at the moment* und *right now* verwendet.

*I'm **reading** this text at the moment.*

What can you see in this photo?
*– A hairdresser. Right now, she's **cutting** a customer's hair.*

B Mit *this week, this month,* usw.
Das *present continuous* kann auch für längere, befristete Handlungen verwendet werden, die gerade stattfinden, z. B. *this week, this month.*

*We**'re visiting** a friend in England this week.*
*Julia **is learning** English on a course in London.*

C Bildung: Aussagen
Das *present continuous* wird mit *to be* und Verb + *-ing* gebildet.

D Bildung: Fragen und Verneinungen
Fragen und Verneinungen werden mit den Frage- und Verneinungsformen von *to be* gebildet.

I'm he's/she's/it's we're you're they're	working	I'm not working she isn't working
		Am I working? Are you working? Are they working?

Verb + *-ing*: Schreibregeln
- An die meisten Verben wird einfach *-ing* angehängt: *work – work**ing**, do – do**ing**.*
- Verben, die auf *-e* enden, verlieren das *-e*: *us**e** – us**ing**, danc**e** – danc**ing**.*
- Kurze Verben, die auf einen Vokal und einen Konsonanten (außer *-y, -w* und *-x)* enden, verdoppeln den Konsonanten: *cu**t** – cu**tting*** (ABER: *pla**y** – pla**ying***).
- Längere Verben, die auf einen Vokal und einen Konsonanten enden, verdoppeln den Konsonanten nicht: *visi**t** – visi**ting**, delive**r** – delive**ring**.* (Ausnahmen: *trave**ll**ing, begi**nn**ing*)
- Bei Verben, die auf *-ie* enden, wird *-ie* zu *-y*: ***ie** – d**y**ing*

***Simple present* oder *present continuous*?**

This is Patrick. He lives in England. He works in a supermarket five days a week.

It's 8.30 in the morning. Patrick is going to the supermarket by bus.

3 Das *simple past*

A Allgemein

Das *simple past* wird verwendet, um Ereignisse in der Vergangenheit zu schildern, die jetzt abgeschlossen sind.
Es wird häufig mit Zeitangaben wie *then, in 1970, last week* und *30 years ago* benutzt.

B Bildung: Aussagen

- Regelmäßige Verben bilden das *simple past* mit *-ed*. Diese Form bleibt in allen Personen gleich.
- Unregelmäßige Verben haben Sonderformen im *simple past* (eine Liste findest du auf dem Klappumschlag). Diese Formen (außer bei *to be*) bleiben ebenfalls in allen Personen gleich.

regelmäßig	**unregelmäßig**	
to work	**to go**	**to be**
I worked	I went	I **was**
he worked	he went	he was
she worked	she went	she was
it worked	it went	it was
we worked	we went	we **were**
you worked	you went	you were
they worked	they went	they were

C Bildung: Fragen und Verneinungen

- Fragen im *simple past* werden in allen Personen mit *did* gebildet.
- Verneinungen bildet man durchgehend mit *didn't*.
- *to be* bildet Fragen und Verneinungen im *simple past* mit eigenen Formen.

Vorsicht!
Nach *did/didn't* steht immer die Grundform des Verbs:
Did he work? (! Did he ~~worked~~?)
She didn't work. (! She didn't ~~worked~~.)

Fragen	**Verneinungen**
Did I work?	I didn't work
Did he/she/it work?	he/she/it didn't work
Did we work?	we didn't work
Did you work?	you didn't work
Did they work?	they didn't work
to be	
Was I?	I wasn't
Was he/she/it?	he/she/it wasn't
Were we/you/they?	we/you/they/weren't

Verb + *-ed*: Schreibregeln

- An die meisten Verben wird einfach *-ed* angehängt: *work – work**ed***.
- An Verben, die auf *-e* enden, hängt man nur *-d* an: ***use** – **used**, dance – dance**d***.
- Kurze Verben, die auf einen Vokal *(a, e, i o, u)* und einen Konsonanten (außer *-y, -w* und *-x*) enden, verdoppeln den Konsonanten: *sho**p** – sho**pp**ed, jo**g** – jo**gg**ed*.
- Längere Verben, die auf einen Vokal und einen Konsonanten enden, verdoppeln den Konsonanten nicht: *visi**t** – visi**t**ed, delive**r** – delive**r**ed*. (Ausnahme: *trave**ll**ed*)
- Bei Verben, die auf *-y* enden, wird *-y* zu *-i*: *stud**y** – stud**ied***.

4 Das *present perfect*

A Allgemein

Mit dem *present perfect* und *since/for* kann man Fragen beantworten, die sich darauf beziehen, wie lange etwas andauert *(How long ...?)*

- *Since* wird mit einem Zeitpunkt (z. B. *2001*, *3 January*, *last year*) benutzt.
- *For* verwendet man für einen Zeitraum (z. B. *two years*, *six months*).

B Bildung: Aussagen

Das *present perfect* wird mit *to have* und der 3. Form (Partizip Perfekt) gebildet.

- Regelmäßige Verben (z. B. *to work*) bilden ihre 3. Form mit *-ed*.
- Unregelmäßige Verben (z. B. *to go*) haben Sonderformen, die in der Liste auf dem Klappumschlag zu finden sind.

I have (I've) he has (he's) she has (she's) it has (it's) we have (we've) you have (you've) they have (they've)	worked gone

C Bildung: Fragen und Verneinungen

Fragen und Verneinungen werden mit Frage- und Verneinungsformen von *to have* + 3. Form des Verbs gebildet.

Have you worked? Has he worked?
I haven't worked he/she/it hasn't worked we/you/they haven't worked

5 Das *past perfect*

A Allgemein

Das *past perfect* wird für ein Ereignis in der Vergangenheit verwendet, das noch vor einem zweiten Ereignis in der Vergangenheit stattfand. Für das länger zurückliegende Ereignis verwendet man das *past perfect*, für das nicht ganz so lange zurückliegende das *simple past*. Wir verwenden das *past perfect* häufig mit *after*.

*She **chose** her job after she **had visited** an interesting company.*

B Bildung

Das *past perfect* wird mit *had* + 3. Form (Partizip Perfekt) des Verbs gebildet. Fragen werden auch mit *had*, Verneinungen mit *hadn't* gebildet.

Aussagen	Verneinungen
I had worked he/she/it had worked we/you/they had worked	I hadn't worked he/she/it hadn't worked we/you/they hadn't worked
Fragen	
Had I worked? Had he/she/it worked? Had we/you/they worked?	

After Jamie had run in the marathon, he went home and went to sleep!

6 Das Futur: *will*

A Allgemein

Will wird für feststehende Ereignisse in der Zukunft sowie für Vorhersagen und Vermutungen verwendet.

*I'**ll have** a family in 10 years.*
*She **won't leave** her job when she has a family.*

B Bildung

- **Aussagen** werden mit *will* + Grundform des Verbs gebildet. Die Kurzform (*'ll*) wird fast immer beim Sprechen und häufig auch beim Schreiben verwendet.
- **Fragen** bildet man, indem man *will* und das Subjekt umstellt. Hier sind die Kurzformen nicht möglich.
- **Verneinungen** werden mit *won't* + Grundform des Verbs gebildet.

I will (I'll) come	Will I come?
he will (he'll) come	Will he come?
she will (she'll) come	Will she come?
it will (it'll) come	Will it come?
we will (we'll) come	Will we come?
you will (you'll) come	Will you come?
they will (they'll) come	Will they come?
I won't come he/she/it won't come we/you/they won't come	

7 Das Futur: *going to*

A Allgemein

Going to verwendet man, um über Pläne und Vorhaben zu sprechen: *I'm going to buy a new jacket* entspricht etwa auf Deutsch: „Ich habe vor, eine neue Jacke zu kaufen."

***I'm going to** have a new job next month.*
***Are** you **going to** leave home?*

B Bildung

- **Aussagen** bildet man mit *to be* + *going to* + Hauptverb.
- **Fragen** bildet man mit den Frageformen von *to be* + *going to* + Hauptverb.
- Für **Verneinungen** benutzt man die Verneinung von *to be* + *going to* + Hauptverb.

I'm he's/she's/it's we're/you're/they're	going to	work
Am I Is he/she/it Are we/you/they	going to	work?
I'm not he/she/it isn't we/you/they aren't	going to	work

Will oder *going to*?

8 Modale Hilfsverben: *must, have to, mustn't* und *don't/doesn't have to*

A Allgemein

Mit den modalen Hilfsverben *must, have to, mustn't* und *don't/doesn't have to* wird ausgedrückt, was man tun muss, nicht tun darf und nicht zu tun braucht (nicht tun muss).

must/have to	**mustn't**	**don't/doesn't have to**
In England you must/have to drive on the left.	You mustn't drive on the right!	He doesn't have to drive! He has a driver.

Must und *have to* haben etwa die gleiche Bedeutung. Sie drücken aus, was man tun **muss.**	*Mustn't* drückt aus, was man **nicht darf**. **Vorsicht!** *Mustn't* bedeutet **nicht** ,nicht müssen'.	*Don't/Doesn't have to* drückt aus, was man **nicht zu tun braucht**. **Vorsicht!** *Don't have to* = nicht müssen.

B Bildung: *must* und *have to*

- *Must* bleibt in allen Personen gleich. Auf *must* folgt die Grundform des Verbs.
- *Have to* bildet man mit *to have* + Grundform des Verbs.

must	**have to**
I must go he/she/it must go we/you/they must go	I have to go he/she/it has to go we/you/they have to go

C Bildung: *mustn't*

Mustn't bleibt ebenfalls bei allen Personen gleich. Auf *mustn't* folgt die Grundform des Verbs.

I mustn't he/she/it mustn't we/you/they mustn't	go

D Bildung: *don't/doesn't have to*

Die Verneinungsform von *have to* bildet man mit *don't/doesn't have to* + Grundform des Verbs.

I don't have to he/she/it doesn't have to we/you/they don't have to	go

9 *If*-Sätze (Bedingungssätze)

A Allgemein

- Ein Bedingungssatz besteht aus einem *if*-Teil und einem Hauptsatz. Der *if*-Teil beschreibt eine Bedingung und der Hauptsatz drückt aus, was passieren wird oder passieren könnte (oder hätte passieren können), wenn diese Bedingung erfüllt wird.
- Bedingungssätze können entweder mit dem *if*-Teil oder mit dem Hauptsatz beginnen. Beginnt ein Satz mit dem *if*-Teil, dann steht immer ein Komma vor dem Hauptsatz.

B *If*-Sätze Typ 1:

***If** you **ask** the robot, it **will clean** the house.*

- Typ 1 drückt aus, was unter bestimmten Bedingungen in der Zukunft geschehen wird oder nicht geschehen wird.

If + simple present	will (not) + verb
If you go to the party,	you'll see Mitch.

C *If*-Sätze Typ 2:

***If** I **worked** for that company, I **would need** a good qualification.*

- Wir benutzen Typ 2, um über eventuelle Situationen zu sprechen oder wenn man bezweifelt, dass eine Bedingung erfüllbar ist.
- **Vorsicht!**
  Anders als im Deutschen darf *would* nur im Hauptsatz, nicht im *if*-Teil stehen.

If + simple past	would(n't) + verb
If you went to the party,	you would see Mitch.

Typ 1: Für Sachen, die passieren werden, wenn ...

Typ 2: Für imaginäre, schwer vorstellbare Situationen

10 Das Passiv

A Allgemein: Aktiv- und Passivsätze

- Aktivsätze betonen, **wer** etwas tut. Passivsätze betonen, **was** getan wird – die Handlung steht im Vordergrund.
- In einem **Aktivsatz** steht das Subjekt vor dem Verb. Gibt es ein Objekt, so steht dieses nach dem Verb.
- **Passivsätze** kann man als ‚umgedrehte' Aktivsätze ansehen: Das Objekt des Aktivsatzes wird zum Subjekt des Passivsatzes.

Aktivsatz

Subjekt	Verb	Objekt
The man	bought	the flowers.

Passivsatz

The man	*bought*	***the flowers.***
The flowers	*were bought*	***by the man.***

B Bildung

- Das Passiv wird mit *to be* + 3. Form des Verbs (Partizip Perfekt) gebildet.

simple present		simple past	
I'm he's she's it's we're you're they're	**made**	I was he was she was it was we were you were they were	**made**

C Mit oder ohne *by*?

Meist wird das Subjekt des Aktivsatzes in einem Passivsatz nicht genannt. Wollen wir aber das Subjekt besonders betonen, können wir es mit *by* am Satzende anfügen. In Satz **1.** ist der Name des Regisseurs besonders wichtig. In Satz **2.** ist es uninteressant, von wem die Blumen angebaut werden.

1. *The film was made* ***by Steven Spielberg****.*
2. *These flowers are grown in* ***Kenya*** *(by ...).*

They delivered oranges to the supermarket yesterday.

Too many oranges were delivered to the supermarket yesterday!

11 Adjektive und Adverbien

A Allgemein

- **Adjektive** beschreiben Personen und Sachen. Sie stehen meist vor einem Substantiv oder nach *to be*.
  *It is a **big** robot.*
  *The robot is **big**.*
- **Adverbien** sagen etwas über Verben aus. Sie sagen uns, **wie** etwas passiert.
  *The robot loads the lorries **quickly**.*

B Adverbien: Bildung

	Adjektiv	Adverb
Ein Adverb wird gebildet, indem *-ly* an das Adjektiv angehängt wird. →	quick	quick**ly**
Bei Adjektiven mit der Endung *-y* wird das *-y* zu *-ily*. →	easy	eas**ily**
Die Endung *-le* wird zu *-ly*. →	simple	simp**ly**
-ic wird zu *-ically*. →	automatic	automat**ically**
Das Adverb von *good* ist *well*. →	good	**well**

12 Relativsätze

A Allgemein

Relativsätze sind Sätze, die eines der Relativpronomen *who*, *which* oder *where* enthalten. Sie beschreiben das Wort, auf das sie sich beziehen, näher.

***The woman who** is helping him is Frau Bliscz.*
***The document which** she has in her hand is Herr Krueger's letter.*

B *who*, *which* oder *where*?

- *who* für Personen
- *which* für Sachen
- *where* für Orte

*A passenger is a person **who** travels by plane.*
*A plane is a machine **which** carries people.*
*The place **where** passengers check in is the check-in desk.*

Vorsicht!
Anders als im Deutschen steht kein Komma vor *who*, *which* und *where*.

Adverbien

Boris can do things very quickly.

Relativsätze

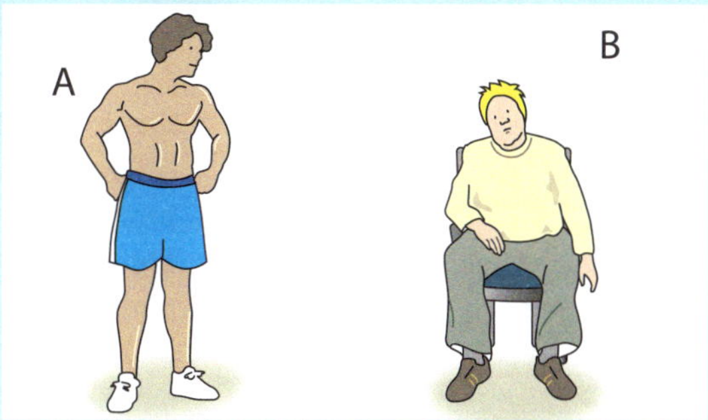

The guy who goes to a fitness club every day is A or B?

Grundwortschatz

Diese Liste umfasst die Vokabeln, die für die Arbeit mit dem Lehr-/Arbeitsbuch *Retail Milestones* vorausgesetzt werden. Da nicht in allen Fällen Mehrfachbedeutungen in der Übersetzung angegeben werden können, ersetzt diese Liste nicht ein umfassendes zweisprachiges Wörterbuch.
Beim Verwenden der Liste als Übersetzungshilfe muss immer der Kontext beachtet werden.
Zahlwörter *(one, two, first, second, ...)*, Pronomen *(I, you, my, your, myself, yourself, ...)*, die Wochentage *(Monday, Tuesday, ...)* sowie die Monatsnamen *(January, February, ...)* sind nicht enthalten.

* = unregelmäßige Verbform

A

a, an ein/e
a little ein wenig
a lot viel/e
about über, um
across (quer) über (hinüber)
address Adresse
after nach, nachdem
afternoon Nachmittag
again wieder
air Luft
airport Flughafen
all alle/s
all right in Ordnung
always immer
a.m. vormittags
and und
animal Tier
to answer antworten
any irgendein/e/er
apple Apfel
around um (herum)
to ask fragen
at an, in, zu
away weg

B

baby Baby
back zurück
bad schlecht
bag Tasche
ball Ball
banana Banane
bank Bank
baseball Baseball
bath Bad
bathroom Badezimmer
to be* sein
beautiful schön
because weil
bed Bett
bedroom Schlafzimmer
before vor, bevor
to begin* anfangen, beginnen
beginning Anfang, Beginn
big groß
bike Fahrrad
bird Vogel
birthday Geburtstag
black schwarz
blue blau
boat Boot
body Körper
book Buch
bottle Flasche
box Karton, Schachtel
boy Junge
bread Brot
to break* (zer)brechen, kaputt machen
breakfast Frühstück
to bring* bringen
brother Bruder
brown braun
building Gebäude
bus Bus
business Geschäft, Business
but aber
to buy* kaufen
by durch, mit

C

cake Kuchen
to call rufen, nennen, heißen
camping Camping
can können
cannot (can't) nicht können
car Auto
careful vorsichtig
to carry tragen
cat Katze
to catch* fangen
centre Zentrum, Mitte
centimetre Zentimeter
chair Stuhl
cheap billig
to check prüfen
cheese Käse
chicken Hähnchen
child Kind
chocolate Schokolade
Christmas Weihnachten
cigarette Zigarette
city Stadt
class Klasse
classroom Klassenzimmer
clean sauber
clever schlau, clever
clock Uhr
closed geschlossen
club Club
coach Reisebus; Trainer/in
coffee Kaffee
cold kalt
colour Farbe
to come* kommen
computer Computer
to cook kochen

correct richtig
to cost* kosten
could könnte/n, konnte/n
country Land
of course (not) natürlich (nicht)
cup Tasse
to cut* schneiden

D

dad Papa
to dance tanzen
date Datum
daughter Tochter
day Tag
dead tot
dear lieb
deep tief
desk Schreibtisch
to dictate diktieren
dictation Diktat
dinner Abendessen
discussion Diskussion
to do* tun, machen
doctor Arzt, Ärztin
dog Hund
door Tür
down (nach) unten
to dream* träumen
dress Kleid
to drink* trinken
to drive* fahren
driver Fahrer/in
dry trocken

E

early früh
east (nach) Osten; östlich
easy leicht
to eat* essen
empty leer; leeren
to end beenden
England England
English englisch
evening Abend
every jede/r/s
exact genau
exam Prüfung
example Beispiel
exercise Übung
to explain erklären
eye Auge

F

face Gesicht
to fall* fallen
false falsch
family Familie
fat dick; fett
father Vater
to feel* fühlen
to fill füllen
to find* finden
film Film
fine gut, schön
finger Finger
to finish aufhören, beenden
first erste/r/s; zuerst
to fish fischen
flower Blume
food Essen, Lebensmittel
foot Fuß
football Fußball
for für
to forget* vergessen
form formen; Form
free frei; kostenlos
friend Freund/in
from von
fruit Frucht
full (of) voll (von, mit)

G

game Spiel
garage Garage
garden Garten
to get* erhalten, bekommen, werden
to get up aufstehen
girl Mädchen
to give* geben
glass Glas
to go* gehen, fahren
gold Gold
good gut
Goodbye. Auf Wiedersehen!
grandfather Großvater
grandmother Großmutter
grass Gras
great groß; großartig
green grün
group Gruppe

H

hair Haar
half halb
happy glücklich
to have* (got) haben
head Kopf
to hear* hören
heavy schwer
hello hallo
to help helfen
here hier
high hoch
hobby Hobby
holiday(s) Ferien, Urlaub
home nach / zu Hause; Zuhause
homework Hausaufgabe(n)
to hope hoffen
hospital Krankenhaus
hot heiß
hotel Hotel
hour Stunde
house Haus
how wie
how much wie viel
how old wie alt
hungry hungrig

I

ice cream Eis
idea Idee
if wenn, falls, ob
ill krank
in in
interest Interesse
interesting interessant
into in (hinein)

J

jacket Jacke
jeans Jeans
job Job

K

to keep* (be)halten
kilo(gramme) Kilo(gramm)
kilometre Kilometer
king König
to kiss küssen
kitchen Küche
to know* wissen

L

lady Dame
late spät
to learn lernen
left links; übrig
lesson Stunde
letter Brief
to lie* (down) (sich hin)legen; liegen
life Leben
light hell; leicht; Licht
to like mögen
line Linie
list Liste
to listen (to) zuhören
litre Liter
little klein; wenig
to live leben, wohnen
living room Wohnzimmer
long lang
to look schauen, (aus)sehen; Blick
to love lieben; Liebe
lucky Glück haben
lunch Mittagessen

M

machine Maschine
to make* machen
man Mann, Mensch
many viele
marmalade Marmelade
metal Metall
metre Meter
middle Mitte
milk Milch
minute Minute
mistake Fehler
moment Moment
money Geld
month Monat
more mehr
morning Morgen
most meiste/r/s
mother Mutter
much viel
mum Mama
music Musik
must müssen

N

name Name
to need brauchen
never nie(mals)
new neu
news Nachricht(en)
newspaper Zeitung
next nächste/r/s
nice schön, nett, gut
night Nacht
no nein; kein
not nicht
nothing nichts
now jetzt
number Zahl, Nummer

O

o'clock Uhr *(Zeitangabe bei vollen Stunden)*
of von, bei, aus
off weg
office Büro
often oft
old alt
one ein/e
only nur
to open öffnen
or oder
to order bestellen; befehlen
other andere/r/s
out aus
over über

P

page Seite
pair Paar
paper Papier
parents Eltern
park Park
partner Partner/in
party Party
passenger Passagier/in
to pay* (be)zahlen
pen Füller; Stift
people Leute
person Person
to phone anrufen
photo Foto
picture Bild
place Ort
to plan planen
plastic (aus) Plastik
to play spielen
play Theaterstück
player Spieler/in
p.m. nachmittags
police Polizei
policeman Polizist
poor arm
pop Pop
post office Post
postcard Postkarte
postman Postbote
to press drücken
pretty hübsch
price Preis
programme Programm
to pronounce aussprechen
to pull ziehen
pupil Schüler/in
to push schieben
to put* stellen, legen, setzen
to put on anziehen; auftragen

Q

queen Königin
question Frage
quick schnell

R

radio Radio
to rain regnen
rainy regnerisch
to read* lesen
to record aufnehmen
red rot
to remember sich erinnern
to repair reparieren
to report berichten
rest Rest
restaurant Restaurant
rich reich
to ride* reiten
right rechts; richtig
to ring* klingeln
river Fluss
road Straße
room Zimmer; Platz
round rund; um (herum)
to run* laufen, rennen

S

sad traurig
safe sicher
same gleiche/r/s
sand Sand
sandwich Sandwich
to say* sagen
school Schule
sea Meer
second zweite/r/s; Sekunde
to see* sehen
to sell* verkaufen
to send* schicken, senden
sentence Satz
ship Schiff
shirt Hemd
shoe Schuh
shop Laden, Geschäft
short kurz
to show* zeigen
side Seite
sing* singen
single einzel/n
sister Schwester
to sit* sitzen
to sleep* schlafen
slow langsam
small klein
to smoke rauchen
so so
sock Socke
soft weich
some etwas, einige
son Sohn
song Lied, Song
(I'm) sorry! Entschuldigung!
soup Suppe
to speak* sprechen
sport Sport
to stand* stehen
to start anfangen
station Bahnhof
to stop aufhören, anhalten
story Geschichte
street Straße
strong stark
stupid dumm
summer Sommer
sun Sonne
supermarket Supermarkt
to swim* schwimmen

T

table Tisch
to take* nehmen, mitnehmen
to talk reden, sprechen
taxi Taxi
tea Tee
to teach* unterrichten
teacher Lehrer/in
team Team
to telephone telefonieren
television Fernseher
to tell* erzählen
text Text
to thank (sich) bedanken
that (one) der / die / das da
the der / die / das
theatre Theater
then dann
there da, dort
these diese
thing Ding
to think* denken, meinen
this diese/r/s
those jene
ticket Fahr-/Eintrittskarte
time Zeit
today heute
together zusammen
toilet Toilette
tomato Tomate
tomorrow morgen
too auch; zu
top Spitze
tourist Tourist/in
town Stadt
to train trainieren
train Zug
to translate übersetzen
tree Baum
trip Reise
trouble Ärger
true richtig; wahr
TV Fernseher

U

uncle Onkel
under unter
to understand* verstehen
until bis
us uns

V

very sehr
to visit besuchen

W

to wake* (up) aufwachen
to walk laufen, gehen
to want wollen
warm warm
to wash waschen
to watch beobachten, anschauen
water Wasser
way Weg
week Woche
weekend Wochenende
well gut; gesund; also
what was
what about was ist mit
when wann
where wo(hin)
which welche/r/s
white weiß
who wer
whole ganz
why warum
will ('ll) werden
to win gewinnen
winter Winter
with mit
woman Frau
word Wort
to work arbeiten
to write* schreiben
to write down aufschreiben
wrong falsch

Y

year Jahr
yes ja
yesterday gestern
young jung

Z

zoo Zoo

Unitbegleitendes Vokabular

Abkürzungen und Zeichen

sb	= somebody
sth	= something
jdm.	= jemandem
jdn.	= jemanden
etw.	= etwas
BE	= britisches Englisch
AE	= amerikanisches Englisch
=	entspricht
≠	entspricht nicht
→	ist das Gegenteil von
↔	ist verwandt mit
!	= Achtung!
1	Vor den Vokabeln finden Sie die jeweiligen Übungsnummern der Unit.

Phonetic alphabet Lautschrift

[:] bedeutet, dass der vorangegangene Laut lang ist
['] bedeutet, dass die folgende Silbe eine Hauptbetonung erhält
[ˌ] bedeutet, dass die folgende Silbe eine Nebenbetonung erhält
[‿] bedeutet, dass die beiden Laute miteinander verbunden werden

[i:]	meet [mi:t]
[ɑ:]	father ['fɑ:ðə]
[ɔ:]	morning ['mɔ:niŋ]
[u:]	blue [blu:]
[ɜ:]	German ['dʒɜ:mən]
[ɪ]	in [ɪn]
[e]	yes [jes]
[æ]	thanks [θæŋks]
[ʌ]	much [mʌtʃ]
[ɒ]	what [wɒt]
[ʊ]	good [gʊd]
[ə]	number ['nʌmbə]
[eɪ]	name [neɪm]
[aɪ]	my [maɪ]
[ɔɪ]	boiled [bɔɪld]
[əʊ]	phone [fəʊn]
[aʊ]	now [naʊ]
[ɪə]	hear [hɪə]
[eə]	where [weə]
[ʊə]	tourist ['tʊərɪst]

[p]	pop [pɒp]
[b]	bye [baɪ]
[t]	town [taʊn]
[d]	drink [drɪŋk]
[k]	coffee ['kɒfɪ]
[g]	good [gʊd]
[tʃ]	church [tʃɜ:tʃ]
[dʒ]	job [dʒɒb]
[f]	fine [faɪn]
[v]	very ['verɪ]
[θ]	thanks [θæŋks]
[ð]	this [ðɪs]
[s]	son [sʌn]
[z]	is [ɪz]
[ʃ]	she [ʃi:]
[ʒ]	television [ˌtelɪ'vɪʒn]
[h]	he [hi:]
[m]	my [maɪ]
[n]	now [naʊ]
[ŋ]	evening ['i:vnɪŋ]
[l]	like ['laɪk]
[r]	room [ru:m]
[w]	we [wi:]
[y]	yes [yes]

Unit 1 Meeting colleagues

	colleague ['kɒli:g]	Kollege/Kollegin	My colleague answers my phone when I'm not at my desk.
A	**Jobs and places of work**		
	place of work [ˌpleɪs‿əv 'wɜ:k]	Arbeitsplatz	I need 20 minutes to get from my home to my place of work.
1	**reason** ['ri:zn]	Grund	Why did you do it? What was the reason?
	next to ['nekst tʊ]	neben	The shoe shop is next to the supermarket.
2	**home-entertainment shop** [ˌhəʊm entə'teɪnmənt ˌʃɒp]	Geschäft für Unterhaltungselektronik	A shop which sells computers, TVs, phones, etc.
B	**Introducing yourself**		
1	**to sum up** [sʌm 'ʌp]	zusammenfassen	Natasha has to sum up the text.
2	**to meet (met, met)** [mi:t, met, met]	(sich) treffen	Let's meet for coffee after school.
	to underline [ˌʌndə'laɪn]	unterstreichen	This is how you <u>underline</u> a word.
	phrase [freɪz]	Redewendung	'Good' is a word, 'to be good at' is a phrase.
	to belong [bɪ'lɒŋ]	gehören (zu)	The shop belongs to me. I am the owner.
	retail chain ['ri:teɪl ˌtʃeɪn]	Einzelhandelskette	Aldi is a large retail chain.
	traineeship [ˌtreɪ'ni:ʃɪp]	Ausbildung	I have just started my traineeship as a shop assistant.
	excited [ɪk'saɪtɪd]	aufgeregt	Tina is very excited about the party tonight.
	to expect [ɪk'spekt]	erwarten	→ expectation
	trainee [ˌtreɪ'ni:]	Auszubildende/r	→ traineeship
	foreign branch [ˌfɒrən 'brɑ:ntʃ]	ausländische Filiale	Deniz works for a foreign branch of the company.
	to pick up [pɪk‿'ʌp]	abholen	My girlfriend picks me up at 6 o'clock every evening.
	entrance ['entrəns]	Eingang	This is the entrance to our shop.
	Pleased to meet you. [ˌpli:zd‿tə 'mi:t‿ju:]	Schön Sie/dich/euch kennen zu lernen.	= Nice to meet you.
	day off [ˌdeɪ‿'ɒf]	freier Tag	Today I don't have to work. I'm having a day off.
	shelf [ʃelf]	Regal	! *plural:* shelves
3	**statement** ['steɪtmənt]	Aussage	→ to state
4	**to complete** [kəm'pli:t]	vervollständigen	Complete the sentences, please.
	to introduce sb to sb [ˌɪntrə'dju:s]	jdn. jdm. vorstellen	I'd like to introduce you to Samira.
C	**Job duties**		
	job duty ['dʒɒb ˌdju:tɪ]	Arbeitsaufgabe	! *plural:* job duties
1	**table** ['teɪbl]	Tabelle	Please fill in the table.
	branch manager ['brɑ:ntʃ ˌmænɪdʒə]	Filialleiter/in	My branch manager is a nice person.

	cashier [kæʃɪə]	Kassierer/in	You can pay the cashier.
	fashion shop ['fæʃn ˌʃɒp]	Modegeschäft	Young people often buy their clothes in fashion shops.
	shop assistant ['ʃɒp‿əˌsɪstnt]	Verkäufer/in	= sales assistant (*AE*), sales clerk (*AE*), salesperson (*AE*)
	company ['kʌmpənɪ]	Firma	I'd like to work for a big computer company.
2	**task** [tɑ:sk]	Aufgabe	My task is to help people.
	to match [mætʃ]	zuordnen	When you match things, you put them together in pairs.
	to serve [sɜ:v]	bedienen	Sometimes I serve customers.
	customer ['kʌstəmə]	Kunde/Kundin	Our customers are usually very friendly.
	to sort [sɔ:t]	sortieren	Every day I have to sort goods.
	to tag [tæg]	auszeichnen	= to label products with prices
	to unpack [ʌn'pæk]	auspacken	↔ to pack
	goods [gʊdz]	Waren	Please send us the goods as soon as possible.

D Talking about yourself and your job

1	**training to become** [bɪ ˌtreɪnɪŋ tʊ bɪ'kʌm]	in der Ausbildung sein zum/zur	He is training to become a shop assistant.
	department [dɪ'pɑ:tmənt]	Abteilung	I work in the fashion department.
	department store [dɪ'pɑ:tmənt ˌstɔ:]	Kaufhaus	The department store is in Königsstraße.
	vocational school [vəʊˌkeɪʃnl 'sku:l]	Berufsschule	On Tuesdays I go to a vocational school.
	once [wʌns]	einmal	I go shopping once a week.
	to have contact with (had, had) [ˌhæv 'kɒntækt wɪð, hæd, hæd]	Kontakt haben mit	Carlos has a lot of contact with customers.
	mood [mu:d]	Stimmung	At work I'm always in a good mood.
	to be afraid [bɪ‿ə'freɪd]	Angst haben	My sister is afraid of the dark.
5	**to take notes (took, taken)** [teɪk 'nəʊts, tʊk, 'teɪkn]	Notizen machen	Listen to the teacher and take notes.

Skills: Practical dictionary work

meaning ['mi:nɪŋ]	Bedeutung	→ to mean
to pass [pɑ:s]	bestehen	When you have passed your driving test you are allowed to drive a car alone.
jewellery ['dʒu:əlrɪ]	Schmuck	Some women wear a lot of jewellery.
reputation [ˌrepjʊ'teɪʃn]	Ruf, Ansehen	She has a good reputation. People think well of her.
to try (on) [traɪ]	(an)probieren	I want to try on this shirt.
search engine ['sɜ:tʃ ˌendʒɪn]	Suchmaschine	→ to search

E Checking

2	**odd one out** [ˌɒd wʌn‿'aʊt]	nicht dazugehören	The odd one out doesn't belong in the group.

Unit 2 Products and services

	service ['sɜ:vɪs]	Dienstleistung	→ to serve

A Describing products

1	**comfortable** ['kʌmftəbl]	bequem	If your shoes are comfortable, they don't hurt your feet when you walk.
	delicious [dɪ'lɪʃəs]	köstlich	This apple is sweet and juicy. It's delicious.
	fashionable ['fæʃnəbl]	modisch	→ fashion → fashion shop
	healthy ['helθɪ]	gesund	→ health
	old-fashioned [ˌəʊld'fæʃnd]	altmodisch	↔ modern
	portable ['pɔ:təbl]	tragbar	A portable TV can be carried from room to room.
	stylish ['staɪlɪʃ]	elegant	→ style
	well-designed [ˌwel dɪ'zaɪnd]	gut gestaltet	= well-made

B Explaining the benefits of products

	benefit ['benɪfɪt]	Nutzen	An advantage a person has from sth.
1	**to decide** [dɪ'saɪd]	entscheiden	Coffee or tea? – I don't know. I can't decide.
	external hard drive [ɪkˌstɜ:nl 'hɑ:d‿draɪv]	externe Festplatte	Sth for storing information from your computer.
	special offer [ˌspeʃl‿'ɒfə]	Sonderangebot	Special offer today: Jeans only £ 15.
	attractive [ə'træktɪv]	attraktiv	→ to attract
	to enter ['entə]	betreten	The teacher enters the classroom.
	to fit [fɪt]	passen	These jeans fit me well.
	to go well with (went, gone) [ˌgəʊ 'wel wɪθ, went, gɒn]	gut passen zu	This shirt goes well with my jeans.
	to suit [su:t]	(jdm.) stehen	You look good in red. Red suits you.
2	**to describe** [dɪ'skraɪb]	beschreiben	→ description
	to guess [ges]	(er)raten	I've no idea what it is. – Well, guess!
	to change [ˌtʃeɪndʒ]	tauschen, wechseln	Now change roles, please.
	to store [stɔ:]	(ab)speichern	If you store sth, you keep it to use later.
4	**to practise** ['præktɪs]	üben	My sister practises her English every day.

C Talking to customers

1	**particularly** [pə'tɪkjʊləlɪ]	besonders	particularly good = especially good
	storage capacity ['stɔ:rɪdʒ kəˌpæsɪtɪ]	Speicherkapazität	→ to store
	actually ['æktʃəlɪ]	eigentlich	! ≠ *aktuell*
	partly ['pɑ:tlɪ]	teilweise	I can partly understand you.
	to offer ['ɒfə]	(an)bieten	→ (on) offer → special offer
	price tag ['praɪs ˌtæg]	Preisschild	A price tag tells you the price of a product.
	hardly ['hɑ:dlɪ]	kaum	! I hardly have time to do my work. = *Ich habe kaum Zeit zum Arbeiten.*
	to compare (with/to) [kəm'peə]	vergleichen (mit)	Compare the two pictures and say what is the same and what is different.

	bargain ['bɑ:gɪn]	Schnäppchen	I'll buy this. It's a real bargain.
	You're welcome. [jɔ:'welkəm]	Bitte schön, gern geschehen.	Thank you. – You're welcome.
	cash desk ['kæʃ ˌdesk]	Kasse	I'll pay for my goods at the cash desk.

D Serving customers successfully

	successfully [sək'sesfəlɪ]	erfolgreich	→ success
1	**sausage** ['sɒsɪdʒ]	Würstchen	Sausage is part of an English breakfast.
	certainly ['sɜ:tənlɪ]	sicherlich	Can you help me? – Certainly, Sir.
	drill [drɪl]	Bohrmaschine	You use a drill to make a hole in sth.
	acceptable [ək'septəbl]	akzeptabel	→ to accept
	change [tʃeɪndʒ]	Wechselgeld	→ to change
	receipt [rɪ'si:t]	Quittung, Kassenzettel	You will get a receipt when you have paid.
2	**to miss** [mɪs]	fehlen, vermissen	I haven't seen my friends this month. I really miss them.

E Checking

2	**to draw (drew, drawn)** [drɔ:, dru:, drɔ:n]	zeichnen	Please draw lines to connect the words.
3	**to enjoy** [ɪn'dʒɔɪ]	genießen	The concert was great. I really enjoyed it.
	cinema ['sɪnəmə]	Kino	Let's go and see the new film at the cinema.

Unit 3 Customers

A Types of customers and their shopping habits

	habit ['hæbɪt]	Gewohnheit	A habit is something that you do regularly.
1	**sceptic** ['skeptɪk]	skeptisch, kritisch	She is a sceptical customer.
	behaviour [bɪ'heɪvjə]	Verhalten	→ to behave
	to distinguish [dɪ'stɪŋgwɪʃ]	unterscheiden	= to find the differences
	environmentally friendly [ɪnˌvaɪərənˌmentəlɪ 'frendlɪ]	umweltfreundlich	= sth that is good for the environment
	to leave (left, left) [li:v, left, left]	(ver)lassen	Don't leave your book here. You need it at school.
	packaging ['pækɪdʒɪŋ]	Verpackung	→ to pack
	carefully ['keəfəlɪ]	sorgfältig	Please read the text carefully.
2	**to identify** [aɪ'dentɪfaɪ]	identifizieren	→ identity
	to take one's time (took, taken) [ˌteɪk wʌnz 'taɪm, tʊk, 'teɪkn]	sich Zeit nehmen	↔ to hurry
	in a hurry [ˌɪn‿ə 'hʌrɪ]	in Eile	to hurry → to hurry up

B Keeping customers satisfied

	to keep sb satisfied (kept, kept) [ki:p ˌsʌmbədɪ 'sætɪsfaɪd, kept, kept]	jdn. zufrieden stellen	I want to keep the customers satisfied.

1	**to adapt** [ə'dæpt]	(sich) anpassen	A shop assistant has to adapt to his/her boss.
	to follow ['fɒləʊ]	folgen	I'll show you where it is. Follow me, please!
	trolley ['trɒlɪ]	Einkaufswagen	I need a trolley for my shopping.
	to study ['stʌdɪ]	studieren, sorgfältig lesen	If you study sth, you learn a lot about it.
	label ['leɪbl]	Etikett	Susan studies the label on her bottle.
	obviously ['ɒbvɪəslɪ]	offensichtlich	He speaks with an accent. He is obviously not from here.
2	**to choose (chose, chosen)** [tʃu:z, tʃəʊz, 'tʃəʊzn]	wählen	→ choice
	DIY-store [ˌdi:aɪ'waɪ ˌstɔ:]	Baumarkt	We bought the materials for our new bathroom in a DIY-store in Dresden.
	pump [pʌmp]	Pumpe	A pump moves water from one place to another.
	kind [kaɪnd]	freundlich	= friendly and good to others
	size [saɪz]	Größe	These jeans are the wrong size.
	guarantee [ˌgærən'ti:]	Garantie	The product comes with a guarantee.
	picture frame ['pɪktʃə ˌfreɪm]	Bilderrahmen	I need a picture frame for my birthday photo.
	to get on sb's nerves (got, got) [ˌget ɒn ˌsʌmbədɪz 'nɜ:vz, gɒt, gɒt]	jdm. auf die Nerven gehen	Sven's girlfriend gets on his nerves.
	to disturb [dɪ'stɜ:b]	stören	Sorry to disturb you.
	kids' zone ['kɪdz‿ˌzəʊn]	Kinderbereich	Your children can play in the kids' zone while you're doing the shopping.
	to take care of (took, taken) [ˌteɪk‿'keər‿əv, tʊk, 'teɪkn]	aufpassen auf	We'll take care of your children.
	elderly ['eldəlɪ]	älter	A more polite word for 'old' (when speaking of people).
	couple ['kʌpl]	Paar	You can call a husband and wife a 'married couple'.

C Different types of shops

1	**specialist shop** ['speʃəlɪst ˌʃɒp]	Fachgeschäft	We always buy our shoes in a specialist shop.
	corner shop ['kɔ:nə ˌʃɒp]	(kleines) Lebensmittelgeschäft	We buy milk in a corner shop near our house.
	far away [ˌfɑ:r‿ə'weɪ]	weit weg	= a long way
	owner ['əʊnə]	Besitzer/in	→ to own
	to collect [kə'lekt]	(ein)sammeln	The shop owner collects all the products and puts them in a bag for me.
	discounter ['dɪskaʊntə]	Billigsupermarkt	At a discounter you can buy products at reduced prices.
	to earn [ɜ:n]	verdienen	When I finish my traineeship I want to earn more money.
	shop fittings ['ʃɒp ˌfɪtɪŋz]	Ladenausstattung	The shop fittings are not important to me.
	to count [kaʊnt]	zählen	It's the price that counts.

	design [dɪ'zaɪn]	Gestaltung	You can find shoes in many different designs in specialist shops.
	advantage [əd'vɑ:ntɪdʒ]	Vorteil	↔ disadvantage
2	**to add** [æd]	hinzufügen	→ additionally
3	**result** [rɪ'zʌlt]	Ergebnis	I hope my exam results will be good.

D Future plans

1	**to take part (took, taken)** [ˌteɪk 'pɑ:t, tʊk, 'teɪkn]	teilnehmen	There are many activities at our school, and it's difficult to decide which ones to take part in.
	survey ['sɜ:veɪ]	Umfrage, Befragung	In a survey you ask people questions.
	married ['mærɪd]	verheiratet	I'm going to be married next year.
5	**showroom** ['ʃəʊru:m]	Ausstellungsraum	The furniture in our showroom is sold later at a discount.
	screen [skri:n]	Bildschirm	You can see texts and pictures on the computer screen.
	fridge [frɪdʒ]	Kühlschrank	A fridge keeps fresh food cool.
6	**development** [dɪ'veləpmənt]	Entwicklung	→ to develop
	to explain [ɪk'spleɪn]	erklären	→ explanation

E Checking

2	**gap** [gæp]	Lücke	Fill in the gaps, please.
3	**to receive** [rɪ'si:v]	empfangen	= to get

Unit 4 Money

A Talking about money

2	**to deal with (dealt, dealt)** ['di:l wɪð, delt, delt]	(be)handeln	If you don't deal with a problem, it won't go away.
	to borrow ['bɒrəʊ]	sich ausleihen	Can I borrow this book from you?
	to count [kaʊnt]	zählen	Please count the money in your cash desk.
	to withdraw (withdrew, withdrawn) [wɪð'drɔ:, wɪð'dru:, wɪð'drɔ:n]	abheben	I must withdraw money from the bank today.
	cash dispenser ['kæʃ dɪˌspensə]	Geldautomat	A cash dispenser is a machine that gives you money.

B Goods and quantities

1	**quantity** ['kwɒntətɪ]	Menge	We sell goods in large quantities.
	a bar of [ə 'bɑ:r‿əv]	eine Tafel	Let's eat a bar of chocolate.
	difference ['dɪfrəns]	Unterschied	There's a big difference in price.
	expensive [ɪk'spensɪv]	teuer	If you stay at an expensive hotel, you'll have to pay a lot of money.
	twice as much as [ˌtwaɪs‿əz 'mʌtʃ‿əz]	zweimal so viel wie	He earns twice as much as his friend.
	honey ['hʌnɪ]	Honig	Tea can be sweetened with honey.
	pineapple ['paɪnæpl]	Ananas	A pineapple is a sweet tropical fruit.
	to have sth left [hæv 'left]	etw. übrig haben	We have a few shirts left.

	completely sold out [kəmˌpliːtlɪ ˌsəʊld ˈaʊt]	vollständig ausverkauft	Our mobile phones are completely sold out.
	a packet of [ə ˈpækɪt‿əv]	eine Packung	We need a packet of washing powder.
	a roll of [ə ˈrəʊl‿əv]	eine Rolle	We also need two rolls of toilet paper.
	a loaf of [ə ˈləʊf‿əv]	ein Laib	! *plural:* loaves
	to have exact change [hæv ɪgˌzækt‿ˈtʃeɪndʒ]	es passend haben	Do you have exact change, Madam?
	carrier bag [ˈkærɪə ˌbæg]	Tragetasche	We need a carrier bag, please.

C Talking about prices

2	**wallet** [ˈwɒlɪt]	Geldbeutel	My money is in my wallet.
	overpriced [ˌəʊvəˈpraɪst]	überteuert	→ price → price tag
	electrical appliance [ɪˌlektrɪkl əˈplaɪəns]	Elektroartikel	A TV is an electrical appliance.
	a good deal [ˌgʊd‿ˈdiːl]	ein gutes Angebot	You can get a good deal on wallets this week.
	leaflet [ˈliːflɪt]	Prospekt	A leaflet is a piece of paper with information about sth.
	to keep one's eyes open (kept, kept) [ˌkiːp wʌnz ˈaɪz ˌəʊpn, kept, kept]	die Augen offen halten	Keep your eyes open for special offers.
	to bargain [ˈbɑːgɪn]	handeln	→ bargain
	leather goods [ˈleðə ˌgʊdz]	Lederwaren	Leather goods are products made of animal skins.
	to be … percent off [bɪ … pəˌsent ˈɒf]	… Prozent weniger kosten	This article is 30 percent off the regular price this week.
	originally [əˈrɪdʒnəlɪ]	ursprünglich	She comes from Britain originally.
	to save [seɪv]	sparen	You can save a lot of money if you look out for special offers.
	taste [teɪst]	Geschmack	→ to taste
	if you don't mind [ɪf jʊ ˌdəʊnt ˈmaɪnd]	wenn es dir/Ihnen nichts ausmacht	If you don't mind, I'll pay for the shopping.
	brand-name product [ˌbrændneɪm ˈprɒdʌkt]	Markenprodukt	= a product made by a particular company
	reduction [rɪˈdʌkʃn]	Ermäßigung	We are offering big reductions today.
	discount [ˈdɪskaʊnt]	Nachlass, Rabatt	→ discounter
3	**to cross out** [krɒs ˈaʊt]	durchstreichen	Please cross out the wrong words.

D At the cash desk

1	**to cancel** [ˈkænsl]	stornieren	Please cancel this receipt.
	repayment [rɪˈpeɪmənt]	Rückzahlung	→ to repay

Skills: Doing internet research

key word [ˈkiː wɜːd]	Stichwort	First you have to think of good key words, then you put them into the search engine.
history [ˈhɪstrɪ]	Geschichte	History is a subject which tells you what happened in the past.

E Checking

1	**announcement** [ə'naʊnsmənt]	Durchsage	An announcement gives people information about what has happened or will happen.

Unit 5 At the department store

A Different floors

1	**floor** [flɔ:]	Stock(werk), Geschoss	Children's wear and toys are on different floors.
	children's wear ['tʃɪldrənz ˌweə]	Kinderbekleidung	= clothes for children
	basement ['beɪsmənt]	Untergeschoss	The food department is in the basement.
	ground floor [ˌgraʊnd 'flɔ:]	Erdgeschoss	The cosmetics department is often on the ground floor.
	top floor [ˌtɒp 'flɔ:]	Obergeschoss	The restaurant is on the top floor.
	to look forward to [lʊk 'fɔ:wəd tu:]	sich freuen auf	I'm looking forward to seeing you tomorrow.
	news [nju:z]	Nachricht(en)	! That's good news. = *Das sind gute Nachrichten./Das ist eine gute Nachricht.*

B Finding products

	lipstick ['lɪpstɪk]	Lippenstift	Many women put lipstick on their lips.
	lunch break ['lʌntʃ ˌbreɪk]	Mittagspause	I always eat a sandwich during my lunch break.
	bright [braɪt]	hell	In the summer the sun is very bright.
	aisle [aɪl]	Gang	I went through the aisles of the supermarket.
	eye shadow ['aɪˌʃædəʊ]	Lidschatten	Women use eye shadow to put colour on their eyelids.
	opposite ['ɒpəzɪt]	gegenüber	The milk is in the same aisle, opposite the washing powder.
	nail polish remover ['neɪl ˌpɒlɪʃ rɪˌmu:və]	Nagellackentferner	→ nail polish
	nail scissors ['neɪl ˌsɪzəz]	Nagelschere	You use nail scissors for cutting your fingernails.

C Finding different departments

1	**information desk** [ˌɪnfə'meɪʃn ˌdesk]	Informationsschalter	→ to inform
	doll [dɒl]	Puppe	You can buy a doll in the toy department.
	downstairs [ˌdaʊn'steəz]	(nach) unten	You have to go to the leather goods department downstairs.
	toy [tɔɪ]	Spielzeug	= sth a child plays with
	barbecue ['bɑ:bɪkju:]	Grillparty	Let's buy some sausages for the barbecue tonight.
	lift [lɪft]	Aufzug	Take a lift to the third floor.
	escalator ['eskəleɪtə]	Rolltreppe	You can use the escalator to go from one floor to another.

	out of order [ˌaʊt‿əv 'ɔ:də]	außer Betrieb	The escalator is out of order. You'll have to use the stairs.
	to repair [rɪ'peə]	reparieren	If sth is broken, you need to repair it.
	to stay [steɪ]	bleiben	You can stay here until it stops raining.
	straight on [streɪt 'ɒn]	geradeaus	Go straight on – don't turn left or right.

D Making comparisons

1	**favour** ['feɪvə]	Gefallen	Can you do me a favour and lend me some money until tomorrow?
	at least [ət‿'li:st]	wenigstens	At least it isn't raining.
	promise ['prɒmɪs]	Versprechen	→ to promise
3	**to remember** [rɪ'membə]	sich erinnern (an)	I must remember Tina's birthday.
	bracket ['brækɪt]	Klammer	These are brackets: (...).

E Checking

1	**to move** [mu:v]	bewegen	Shall I move the goods closer to the door?

Unit 6 Sales promotion

	sales promotion ['seɪlzprə'məʊʃn]	Verkaufsförderung	→ to promote

A The history of a company

1	**public relations** [ˌpʌblɪk rɪ'leɪʃnz]	Öffentlichkeitsarbeit	Please talk to a person from our public relations department.
	can [kæn]	Dose	You can buy cola in cans or in bottles.
	to invent [ɪn'vent]	erfinden	→ inventor
	pharmacist ['fɑ:məsɪst]	Apotheker/in	→ pharmacy
	famous ['feɪməs]	berühmt	A lot of people know who David Beckham is. He is very famous.
	state [steɪt]	Staat	= country or part of a country
	businessman ['bɪznɪsmən]	Geschäftsmann	! *plural:* businessmen; → businesswoman

B Planning a product promotion

1	**flyer** ['flaɪə]	Werbeblatt	People often get promotion flyers which advertise products.
	to introduce [ˌɪntrə'dju:s]	einführen	We will introduce a new model next year.
	to cope with ['kəʊp wɪð]	fertig werden mit	We can cope with such a problem.
	challenge ['tʃælɪndʒ]	Herausforderung	His job is a daily challenge.
	to resist [rɪ'zɪst]	widerstehen	I can't resist this really good offer.
	to invite [ɪn'vaɪt]	einladen	→ invitation
	to celebrate ['seləbreɪt]	feiern	How do you celebrate your birthday? – I usually have a party.
	launch [lɔ:ntʃ]	Start	The launch of the campaign will be next week.
	competition [ˌkɒmpə'tɪʃn]	Wettbewerb	He wants to win the competition.

prize [praɪz]	Preis(gewinn)	You can win a prize for the best project.
five-star hotel [ˌfaɪvstɑː həʊ'tel]	5-Sterne Hotel	We can spend the night in a five-star hotel.

C **Convincing and binding customers**

	to convince [kən'vɪns]	überzeugen	We can't convince her. She doesn't believe us.
	to bind (bound, bound) [baɪnd, baʊnd, baʊnd]	(an sich) binden	A shop wants to bind customers.
1	**mobile phone** [ˌməʊbaɪl 'fəʊn]	Handy	! *Im Englischen bezeichnet man ein Mobiltelefon nicht als ‚Handy'.*
	campaign [kæm'peɪn]	Kampagne	We are having a campaign to advertise mobile phones.
	background ['bækgraʊnd]	Hintergrund	The background of the picture is very dark.
	engineer [ˌendʒɪ'nɪə]	Ingenieur/-in	My father builds bridges. He's an engineer.
	production [prə'dʌkʃn]	Herstellung	→ to produce → producer
	text messaging ['tekst ˌmesɪdʒɪŋ]	Textmitteilung	The first mobile phones had no text messaging.
	to weigh [weɪ]	wiegen	→ weight
	to demonstrate ['demənstreɪt]	*hier:* vorführen	Let me demonstrate how it works.
	to increase ['ɪnkriːs]	zunehmen	↔ decrease
3	**to advertise** ['ædvətaɪz]	Werbung machen	→ advertise(ment)
	to deliver [dɪ'lɪvə]	(aus)liefern	When can you deliver the goods?
	earphone ['ɪəfəʊn]	Ohrhörer	We can offer you earphones, too. Then you can listen to music without other people hearing it.
	flat rate ['flætreɪt]	einheitlicher Kostensatz	We have a flat rate for local phone calls.
	soldier ['səʊldʒə]	Soldat/in	It is a soldier's job to fight, usually for his/her country.
	to station ['steɪʃn]	stationieren	A lot of foreign soldiers are stationed in Germany.
	to include [ɪn'kluːd]	beinhalten	The price includes all drinks.
	period of time [ˌpɪərɪəd‿əv 'taɪm]	Zeitraum	We will sell this product over a long period of time.
	angry ['æŋgrɪ]	wütend	He got very angry with the shop assistant.
	bill [bɪl]	Rechnung	The bill shows you how much you have to pay for sth.
4	**unsure** [ʌn'ʃɔː]	unsicher	→ sure
7	**to agree** [ə'griː]	sich einigen	We agreed on a plan.
	target group ['tɑːgɪt ˌgruːp]	Zielgruppe	The target group for this product is teenagers.

Skills: Describing a picture

foreground ['fɔːgraʊnd]	Vordergrund	↔ background

Unit 7 Special sales situations

A Handling goods

1	**to handle** ['hændl]	handhaben	= to deal with
	to be allowed to [bɪ‿ə'laʊd‿tʊ]	dürfen	= may
	to touch [tʌtʃ]	anfassen	Don't touch that! It's very hot!
	to smell [smel]	riechen	→ smell
	fragile ['frædʒaɪl]	zerbrechlich	Usually glass is very fragile.
	carpet ['kɑ:pɪt]	Teppich(boden)	We have a new carpet in our living room.
	sample ['sɑ:mpl]	Muster	This is a sample of a new perfume.

B Giving instructions

1	**credit card** ['kredɪt ˌkɑ:d]	Kreditkarte	It is not possible to pay by credit card in this shop.
2	**button** ['bʌtn]	Knopf	It's easy to take a photo – just press the button.
	to go wrong (went, gone) [ˌgəʊ 'rɒŋ, went, gɒn]	schiefgehen	Oh no! Everything went wrong today.
	to go off (went, gone) [gəʊ‿'ɒf, went, gɒn]	schlecht werden	This milk has gone off.
	travel guide ['trævl ˌgaɪd]	Reiseführer	A travel guide helps people to find their way when they are visiting new places.
3	**rule** [ru:l]	Regel	Can you find a rule for the plural forms?
4	**care instruction** ['keə ɪnˌstrʌkʃn]	Pflegehinweis	Care instructions tell you how to look after certain products.
	to bleach [bli:tʃ]	bleichen	This tablecloth looks awful and grey. I will bleach it.
	to iron [aɪən]	bügeln	Your shirt looks terrible. You have to iron it.
	heat [hi:t]	Hitze	→ hot
	flammable ['flæməbl]	entflammbar	This material is extremely flammable. It burns very easily.
	to protect [prə'tekt]	schützen	→ protection
	humidity [hju:'mɪdɪtɪ]	Feuchtigkeit	Today there's going to be sunshine and high humidity.

C Explaining rules and regulations

	regulation [ˌregjə'leɪʃn]	Vorschrift	There are many regulations at school.
1	**to keep (kept, kept)** [ki:p, kept, kept]	sich halten (an)	Please keep to the rules!
	polite [pə'laɪt]	höflich	It is polite to say thank you when you get a present.
	unfortunately [ˌʌn'fɔ:tʃnətlɪ]	leider	↔ fortunately
	smoking area ['sməʊkɪŋ ˌeərɪə]	Raucherzone	↔ non-smoking area
	dirty ['dɜ:tɪ]	dreckig	Your jacket is dirty. You should put it in the washing machine.
	condition [kən'dɪʃn]	Zustand	You must keep the product in good condition.
	pet [pet]	Haustier	You can have a cat or a dog as a pet.

	purchase ['pɜ:tʃəs]	Einkauf	Purchases over € 50 are delivered free of charge.

D Dealing with customer complaints

	complaint [kəm'pleɪnt]	Beschwerde	→ to complain
1	**to appreciate** [ə'pri:ʃieɪt]	schätzen	If you appreciate sth, then you think highly of it.
	exception [ɪk'sepʃn]	Ausnahme	You can put your mobile phones on your desks. Today, I'll make an exception.
	to exchange [ɪks'tʃeɪndʒ]	(um)tauschen	I'm very unhappy with this product. I would like to exchange it for another one.
	replacement [rɪ'pleɪsmənt]	Ersatz	→ to replace
	return [rɪ'tɜ:n]	Rückgabe	Some department stores don't accept any returns.
	to ruin ['ru:ɪn]	ruinieren	I walked through the rain. Now my hair is ruined.
	suggestion [sə'dʒestʃn]	Vorschlag	Can I make a suggestion? Let's go home.
	voucher ['vaʊtʃə]	Gutschein	We can give you a voucher which you can use in our shop.
	glove [glʌv]	Handschuh	Gloves keep your hands warm in the winter.
	upset [ʌp'set]	aufgebracht	= very unhappy or worried
	to see a point (saw, seen) [ˌsi:‿ə 'pɔɪnt, sɔ:, si:n]	einen Standpunkt verstehen	I can see your point.
2	**dissatisfied** [dɪs'sætɪsfaɪd]	unzufrieden	↔ satisfied
	to solve [sɒlv]	lösen	→ solution
3	**to praise** [preɪz]	loben	↔ to criticise
	scratch [skrætʃ]	Kratzer	There is a big scratch on the front door.
	to recommend [ˌrekə'mend]	empfehlen	Can you recommend a good mobile phone?

E Convincing upset customers

1	**to calm down** [kɑ:m 'daʊn]	beruhigen	= to relax
	to lose (lost, lost) [lu:z, lɒst, lɒst]	verlieren	I can't find my wallet. I must have lost it.
	inconvenience [ˌɪnkən'vi:nɪəns]	Unannehmlichkeit	I'm sorry for causing any inconvenience.
	content ['kɒntent]	Inhalt	The content of the report is important.
	from abroad [frəm ə'brɔ:d]	aus dem Ausland	Tomorrow we will have guests from abroad.
	to get right (got, got) [get 'raɪt, gɒt, gɒt]	richtig verstehen	= to understand
	to repeat [rɪ'pi:t]	wiederholen	= to say (or do) sth again

F Checking

1	**to burn (burnt, burnt)** [bɜ:n, bɜ:nt, bɜ:nt]	(ver)brennen	Marcus burnt his hand because he put it in the fire.
2	**to lock** [lɒk]	abschließen	→ lock

Unit 8 After-sales services

A Product recall

	recall ['ri:kɔ:l]	Rückrufaktion	→ to recall
1	**to damage** ['dæmɪdʒ]	beschädigen	The storm damaged our shop window.
	in the long run [ɪn ðə 'lɒŋ ˌrʌn]	auf lange Sicht	I think you will do well at school in the long run.
	construction fault [kən'strʌkʃn ˌfɒlt]	Konstruktionsfehler	The product doesn't work properly because it has a construction fault.
	to explode [ɪk'spləʊd]	explodieren	If a tin of peas has gone off, it might explode when you open it.
2	**trust** ['trʌst]	Vertrauen	The quality of this product is so bad that I have lost trust in it.
	to unsettle [ʌn'setl]	beunruhigen	A product recall can unsettle customers.

B Dealing with product recalls

1	**press release** ['pres rɪˌli:s]	Pressemitteilung	There is a press release about the new film in the newspaper.
	bathroom scale [ˌbɑ:θru:m 'skeɪl]	Gewichtswaage	I always weigh myself on the bathroom scale before I go to bed.
	helpline ['helplaɪn]	telefonischer Beratungsdienst	Please call our helpline to get more information.
	item ['aɪtəm]	Artikel	The item costs € 15.
	refund ['ri:fʌnd]	Rückerstattung	→ to refund
	to apologise [ə'pɒlədʒaɪz]	sich entschuldigen	= to say sorry
	compensation [ˌkompen'seɪʃn]	Schadensersatz	Big department stores usually offer compensation for damaged goods.
	to spend (spent, spent) [spend, spent, spent]	ausgeben	I spent all my pocket money on clothes last month. I spend more time on reading than on sport.
	to meet sb's needs (met, met) [mi:t ˌsʌmbədɪz 'ni:dz, met, met]	die Bedürfnisse von jdm. befriedigen	Our shop tries to meet our customers' needs.

C Customer feedback

1	**furniture** ['fɜ:nɪtʃə]	Möbel	! The furniture is new. = *Die Möbel sind neu.*
	on time [ɒn 'taɪm]	pünktlich	When you arrive on time, you arrive exactly at the right time.
	to share [ʃeə]	teilen	It is nice to share things with friends.
2	**past** [pɑ:st]	vorbei	I didn't go into the leather department. I just walked past it.

D Dealing with complaints and apologising

1	**customer service** [ˌkʌstəmə 'sɜ:vɪs]	Kundendienst	We offer an excellent customer service.
	suitcase ['su:tkeɪs]	Koffer	Have you packed your suitcase?
	to rely on [rɪ'laɪ‿ɒn]	sich verlassen auf	People can rely on this information.
	to expect [ɪk'spekt]	erwarten	We are expecting many customers this afternoon.
3	**signature** ['sɪgnətʃə]	Unterschrift	→ to sign

salutation [ˌsæljʊ'teɪʃn]	Anrede	A greeting at the beginning of a letter.
subject line ['sʌbdʒekt ˌlaɪn]	Betreffzeile	Here you say in a few words what the letter is about.
reference line ['refrəns ˌlaɪn]	Bezugszeichenzeile	The reference line gives information about the customer and the company.
in the meantime [ɪn ðə 'mi:ntaɪm]	in der Zwischenzeit	My colleague will be here in a minute. In the meantime please sit down.
to enclose [ɪn'kləʊz]	beilegen	If you enclose sth, you put it in with the letter you want to send.

Skills: Interpreting diagrams

to illustrate ['ɪləstreɪt]	veranschaulichen	Let me illustrate this with an example.
countable ['kaʊntəbl]	zählbar	↔ uncountable
leisure time [ˌleʒətaɪm]	Freizeit	Football is my favourite leisure time activity.
bar chart ['bɑ: ˌtʃɑ:t]	Balkendiagramm	Please use the bar chart and analyse the pupils' leisure time activities.
percentage [pə'sentɪdʒ]	Prozentsatz	→ percent

E Checking

1	**fair trade** [ˌfeə 'treɪd]	fairer Handel	Some shops sell fair-trade coffee and chocolate.

Unit 9 Getting goods delivered

A Making an enquiry

	enquiry [ɪn'kwaɪərɪ]	Anfrage	We would like to make an enquiry.
1	**supplier** [sə'plaɪə]	Lieferant	Sb who provides things that people want or need.
	to interrupt [ˌɪntə'rʌpt]	unterbrechen	If you interrupt sb, you speak while he/she is talking.
	wristwatch ['rɪstwɒtʃ]	Armbanduhr	A watch which you wear around your wrist.

B A business letter

1	**with reference to** [wɪð 'refrəns tu:]	mit Bezug auf	With reference to your offer of 6 February, we would like to order five dresses, model BE5, in sizes 32 to 40.
	to request [rɪ'kwest]	bitten	= to ask for sth politely
	to extend [ɪk'stend]	erweitern	= to make sth longer or larger
	range of products [ˌreɪndʒ‿əv 'prɒdʌkts]	Produktpalette	We want to extend our range of products.
	trade discount [ˌtreɪd‿'dɪskaʊnt]	Handelsnachlass/rabatt	Most companies offer trade discounts for large orders.
	terms of delivery and payment [ˌtɜ:mz‿əv dɪˌlɪvərɪ‿ən 'peɪmənt]	Lieferungs- und Zahlungsbedingungen	→ to deliver
	to grow (grew, grown) [grəʊ, gru:, grəʊn]	wachsen	There is a growing market for these products.

	in advance [ɪn‿əd'vɑːns]	im Voraus	If you want to be sure that you'll get the mobile phones, then order them in advance, please.
	reply [rɪ'plaɪ]	Antwort	= answer
5	**complimentary close** [ˌkɒmplɪmentrɪ 'kləʊz]	Grußformel	You finish a letter with a complimentary close.

C Receiving an offer

1	**encs = enclosures** [ɪn'kləʊʒəz]	Anhang	Sth that you include with a letter.
	further ['fɜːðə]	weiter	We can give you a further discount.
	cash discount [ˌkæʃ 'dɪskaʊnt]	Barzahlungsrabatt, Skonto	We can also offer you a cash discount.
	settlement ['setlmənt]	Bezahlung	We will accept settlement by Monday next week.
	to desire [dɪ'zaɪə]	wünschen	Our company has the products that your customers desire.
	in stock [ɪn 'stɒk]	vorrätig	My father has a lot of batteries in stock at home.
	order ['ɔːdə]	Bestellung	→ to order
	according to [ə'kɔːdɪŋ tuː]	gemäß	According to our telephone conversation, I'll send you a written enquiry.
	to dispatch [dɪ'spætʃ]	abschicken	Please dispatch our order tomorrow.
	free of charge [ˌfriː‿əv 'tʃɑːdʒ]	kostenlos	We will deliver the goods free of charge.
	air mail ['eə ˌmeɪl]	Luftpost	We will send the goods by air mail.
	receipt of order [rɪˌsiːt‿əv 'ɔːdə]	Auftragseingang	My boss will call you again after receipt of order.

D Placing an order

	to place [pleɪs]	*hier:* erteilen	We are very pleased to place our order with you.
1	**to grant** [grɑːnt]	gewähren	We will grant you a discount.

E Delivery and payment

1	**to confirm** [kən'fɜːm]	bestätigen	→ confirmation
	to remind [rɪ'maɪnd]	erinnern	My colleague reminded me about the meeting with the branch manager.
	bank transfer ['bæŋk ˌtrænsfɜː]	Banküberweisung	You will have to pay by bank transfer.
2	**in cash** [ɪn 'kæʃ]	in bar	We paid for the journey in cash.
	in instalments [ɪn ɪn'stɔːlmənts]	in Raten	The price of the computer is very high. Are we allowed to pay in instalments?
	on receipt [ɒn rɪ'siːt]	bei Erhalt	We will dispatch the goods on receipt of your payment.
	invoice ['ɪnvɔɪs]	Rechnung	The subscription should be paid for on receipt of the invoice.
	subscription [səb'skrɪpʃn]	Abonnement	We can offer you a subscription to a news magazine.
3	**air freight** ['eə ˌfreɪt]	Luftfracht	Large goods are sent by air freight, small goods by air mail.

Skills: Commercial correspondence

	to improve [ɪm'pruːv]	verbessern	When you improve your English, your English gets better.

F Checking

1	**grid** [grɪd]	Gitter	The words from top to bottom cross with the words from left to right in the following grid.

Unit 10 Job hunting

	to hunt [hʌnt]	*hier:* suchen	After finishing school I will have to hunt for the right job.

A Which job?

1	**to fire** ['faɪə]	entlassen	The company fired a lot of people last year.
	letter of application [ˌletər‿əv‿ˌæplɪ'keɪʃn]	Bewerbungsschreiben	→ to apply → applicant
	career [kə'rɪə]	Karriere	I want to build a good career.
	to give up (gave, given) [gɪv‿'ʌp, geɪv, 'gɪvn]	aufgeben	Try again, don't give up!
	job centre ['dʒɒb ˌsentə]	Arbeitsamt	If you are unemployed, you must go to the local job centre in your town.

B Looking at job adverts

1	**mark** [mɑːk]	Note	Aynur always gets good marks at school.
	to employ [ɪm'plɔɪ]	beschäftigen, einstellen	→ employer
	currently ['kʌrəntlɪ]	zur Zeit	She is currently working for us.
	temporary job [ˌtemprərɪ 'dʒɒb]	befristete Stelle	The department store can offer you a temporary job.
	part-time (*adj*), **part time** (*adv*) [ˌpɑːt‿taɪm; ˌpɑːt‿'taɪm]	Teilzeit	I work 15 hours a week. It's a part-time job.
	full-time (*adj*), **full time** (*adv*) [ˌfʊltaɪm; ˌfʊl'taɪm]	Vollzeit	I work 40 hours per week. It's a full-time job.
	fully qualified [ˌfʊlɪ 'kwɒlɪfaɪd]	voll qualifiziert	→ to qualify → qualification

C Writing a letter of application

1	**personnel manager** [ˌpɜːsən'el ˌmænɪdʒə]	Personalchef	You should send your application to the personnel manager.
	CV (= curriculum vitae) [ˌsiː'viː]	Lebenslauf	A CV describes the jobs and activities that you have done, your school education, etc.
	to attend [ə'tend]	besuchen	Did you attend the conference? = Were you at the conference?
	job interview ['dʒɒb ˌɪntəvjuː]	Bewerbungsgespräch	I'm invited for a job interview.

D Writing a CV

1 **work experience** ['wɜ:k ɪkˌspɪərɪəns]	Berufserfahrung	→ experience
education [ˌedjʊ'keɪʃn]	Ausbildung	What can you tell me about your education?
secondary school ['sekəndrɪ ˌsku:l]	weiterführende Schule	My older brother attends a secondary school.
primary school ['praɪmərɪ ˌsku:l]	Grundschule	My little sister goes to primary school.
mother tongue [ˌmʌðə 'tʌŋ]	Muttersprache	The language which your parents have taught you.
driving licence ['draɪvɪŋ ˌlaɪsəns]	Führerschein	When you have passed your driving test, then you are given a driving licence.

E A job interview

2 **subject** ['sʌbdʒɪkt]	Fach	My favourite subject is English.

Skills: Applying for a job

journey ['dʒɜ:nɪ]	Reise	On our journey through England we met a lot of nice people.
upright ['ʌpraɪt]	aufrecht	You must sit upright during a job interview.
truth ['tru:θ]	Wahrheit	My girlfriend never told me the truth in the past.
to lie [laɪ]	lügen	↔ to tell the truth

Activity pages

Role play: Different lives

previous ['pri:vɪəs]	vorherig	I earned less at my previous job than at my current job.
to hit (hit, hit) [hɪt, hɪt, hɪt]	schlagen	Tom hit me yesterday. He is no longer my friend.

Communicative crossword

clue [klu:]	Hinweis	I don't know the answer. Give me a clue, please.

Talking about statistics

graph [grɑ:f]	Diagramm	A kind of diagram which is often used in maths.
figure ['fɪgə]	Zahl	We had high sales figures last year.
to rise (rose, risen) [raɪz, rəʊz, 'rɪzn]	steigen	Sales always rise in December.
gradual ['grædʒʊəl]	allmählich	A gradual change is a slow change.
sharp [ʃɑ:p]	scharf	There has been a sharp increase in sales.

Alphabetisches Wörterverzeichnis

In dieser alphabetischen Wortliste ist das gesamte Vokabular aus dem unitbegleitenden Wörterverzeichnis enthalten. Die Angaben hinter den Einträgen geben die Fundstelle an (z.B. 22 = Seite 22, AP = Activity pages).

A

acceptable [əkˈsɛptəbl] akzeptabel 17
according to [əˈkɔ:dɪŋ tu:] gemäß 72
actually [ˈæktʃəlɪ] eigentlich 16
to adapt [əˈdæpt] sich anpassen 22
to add [æd] hinzufügen 24
advantage [ədˈvɑ:ntɪdʒ] Vorteil 24
to advertise [ˈædvətaɪz] Werbung machen 48
to agree [əˈgri:] sich einigen 50
air freight [ˈeə ˌfreɪt] Luftfracht 74
air mail [ˈeə ˌmeɪl] Luftpost 72
aisle [aɪl] Gang 38
angry [ˈæŋgrɪ] wütend 48
announcement [əˈnaʊnsmənt] Durchsage 35
to apologise [əˈpɒlədʒaɪz] sich entschuldigen 62
to appreciate [əˈpri:ʃɪeɪt] schätzen 56
at least [ət ˈli:st] wenigstens 40
to attend [əˈtend] teilnehmen 79
attractive [əˈtræktɪv] attraktiv 14

B

background [ˈbækgraʊnd] Hintergrund 47
bank transfer [ˈbæŋk ˌtrænsfɜ:] Banküberweisung 73
bar chart [ˈbɑ: ˌtʃɑ:t] Balkendiagramm 66
a bar of [ə ˈbɑ:r‿əv] eine Tafel 30
barbecue [ˈbɑ:bɪkju:] Grillparty 39
to bargain [ˈbɑ:gɪn] handeln 32
bargain [ˈbɑ:gɪn] Schnäppchen 16
basement [ˈbeɪsmənt] Untergeschoss 37
bathroom scale [ˌbɑ:θru:m ˈskeɪl] Gewichtswaage 62
to be ... percent off [bɪ ... pəˌsent ˈɒf] ... Prozent weniger kosten 33
to be afraid [bɪ‿əˈfreɪd] Angst haben 9
to be allowed to [bɪ‿əˈlaʊd‿tʊ] dürfen 53
behaviour [bɪˈheɪvjə] Verhalten 21
to belong [bɪˈlɒŋ] gehören (zu) 6
benefit [ˈbenɪfɪt] Nutzen 14
bill [bɪl] Rechnung 48
to bind (bound, bound) [baɪnd, baʊnd, baʊnd] (an sich) binden 47
to bleach [bli:tʃ] bleichen 54
to borrow [ˈbɒrəʊ] sich ausleihen 29
bracket [ˈbrækɪt] Klammer 42
branch manager [ˈbrɑ:ntʃ ˌmænɪdʒə] Filialleiter/in 8
brand-name product [ˌbrændneɪm ˈprɒdʌkt] Markenprodukt 33
bright [braɪt] hell 38
to burn (burnt, burnt) [bɜ:n, bɜ:nt, bɜ:nt] (ver)brennen 59
businessman [ˈbɪznɪsmən] Geschäftsmann 45
button [ˈbʌtn] Knopf 54

C

to calm down [kɑ:m ˈdaʊn] sich beruhigen 58
campaign [kæmˈpeɪn] Kampagne 47
can [kæn] Dose 45
to cancel [ˈkænsl] stornieren 34
care instruction [ˈkeə ɪnˌstrʌkʃn] Pflegehinweis 54
career [kəˈrɪə] Karriere 77
carefully [ˈkeəfəlɪ] sorgfältig 21
carpet [ˈkɑ:pɪt] Teppich(boden) 53
carrier bag [ˈkærɪə ˌbæg] Tragetasche 30
cash desk [ˈkæʃ ˌdesk] Kasse 16
cash discount [ˌkæʃ ˈdɪskaʊnt] Barzahlungsrabatt, Skonto 72
cash dispenser [ˈkæʃ dɪˌspensə] Geldautomat 29
cashier [kæʃˈɪə] Kassierer/in 8
to celebrate [ˈseləbreɪt] feiern 46
certainly [ˈsɜ:tnlɪ] sicherlich 17
challenge [ˈtʃælɪndʒ] Herausforderung 46
change [tʃeɪndʒ] Wechselgeld 17
to change [tʃeɪndʒ] tauschen, wechseln 15
children's wear [ˈtʃɪldrənz ˌweə] Kinderbekleidung 37
to choose (chose, chosen) [tʃu:z, tʃəʊz, ˈtʃəʊzn] wählen 23
cinema [ˈsɪnəmə] Kino 19
clue [klu:] Hinweis AP
colleague [ˈkɒli:g] Kollege/Kollegin 5
to collect [kəˈlekt] (ein)sammeln 24
comfortable [ˈkʌmftəbl] bequem 13
company [ˈkʌmpənɪ] Firma 8
to compare (with/to) [kəmˈpeə] vergleichen (mit) 16
compensation [ˌkompenˈseɪʃn] Schadensersatz 62
competition [ˌkɒmpəˈtɪʃn] Wettbewerb 46
complaint [kəmˈpleɪnt Beschwerde 56
to complete [kəmˈpli:t] vervollständigen 7
completely sold out [kəmˌpli:tlɪ ˌsəʊld ˈaʊt] vollständig ausverkauft 30

complimentary close [ˌkɒmplɪmentrɪ 'kləʊz] Grußformel 71
condition [kən'dɪʃn] Zustand 55
to confirm [kən'fɜ:m] bestätigen 73
construction fault [kən'strʌkʃn ˌfɒlt] Konstruktionsfehler 61
content ['kɒntent] Inhalt 58
to convince [kən'vɪns] überzeugen 47
to cope with ['kəʊp wɪð] fertig werden mit 46
corner shop ['kɔ:nə ˌʃɒp] (kleines) Lebensmittelgeschäft 24
to count [kaʊnt] zählen 29
countable ['kaʊntəbl] zählbar 66
couple ['kʌpl] Paar 23
credit card ['kredɪt ˌkɑ:d] Kreditkarte 54
to cross out [krɒs 'aʊt] durchstreichen 33
currently ['kʌrəntlɪ] zur Zeit 78
customer ['kʌstəmə] Kunde/Kundin 8
customer service [ˌkʌstəmə 'sɜ:vɪs] Kundendienst 64
CV (= curriculum vitae) [ˌsi:'vi:] Lebenslauf 79

D

to damage ['dæmɪdʒ] beschädigen 61
day off [ˌdeɪ‿'ɒf] freier Tag 6
to deal (with) (dealt, dealt) ['di:l wɪð, delt, delt] sich befassen mit 29
to decide [dɪ'saɪd] entscheiden 14
delicious [dɪ'lɪʃəs] köstlich 13
to deliver [dɪ'lɪvə] (aus)liefern 48
to demonstrate ['demənstreɪt] *hier:* vorführen 47
department [dɪ'pɑ:tmənt] Abteilung 9
department store [dɪ'pɑ:tmənt ˌstɔ:] Kaufhaus 9
to describe [dɪ'skraɪb[beschreiben 15
design [dɪ'zaɪn] Gestaltung 24
to desire [dɪ'zaɪə] wünschen 72
development [dɪ'veləpmənt] Entwicklung 26
difference ['dɪfrəns] Unterschied 30
dirty ['dɜ:tɪ] dreckig 55
discount ['dɪskaʊnt] Nachlass, Rabatt 33
discounter ['dɪskaʊntə] Billigsupermarkt 24
to dispatch [dɪ'spætʃ] abschicken 72
dissatisfied [dɪs'sætɪsfaɪd] unzufrieden 56
to distinguish [dɪ'stɪŋgwɪʃ] unterscheiden 21
to disturb [dɪ'stɜ:b] stören 23
DIY-store [ˌdi:aɪ'waɪ ˌstɔ:] Baumarkt 23
doll [dɒl] Puppe 39
downstairs [ˌdaʊn'steəz] (nach) unten 39
to draw (drew, drawn) [drɔ:, dru:, drɔ:n] zeichnen 19
drill [drɪl] Bohrmaschine 17
driving licence ['draɪvɪŋ ˌlaɪsəns] Führerschein 80

E

to earn [ɜ:n] verdienen 24
earphone ['ɪəfəʊn] Ohrhörer 48
education [ˌedjʊ'keɪʃn] Ausbildung 80
elderly ['eldəlɪ] älter 23
electrical appliance [ɪˌlektrɪkl ə'plaɪəns] Elektroartikel 32
to employ [ɪm'plɔɪ] beschäftigen, einstellen 78
to enclose [ɪn'kləʊz] beilegen 65
encs = enclosures [ɪn'kləʊʒəz] Anhang 72
engineer [ˌendʒɪ'nɪə] Ingenieur/in 47
to enjoy [ɪn'dʒɔɪ] genießen 19
enquiry [ɪn'kwaɪərɪ] Anfrage 69
to enter ['entə] betreten 14
entrance ['entrəns] Eingang 6
environmentally friendly [ɪnˌvaɪərənˌmentəlɪ 'frendlɪ] umweltfreundlich 21
escalator ['eskəleɪtə] Rolltreppe 39
exception [ɪk'sepʃn] Ausnahme 56
to exchange [ɪks'tʃeɪndʒ] (um)tauschen 56
excited [ɪk'saɪtɪd] aufgeregt 6
to expect [ɪk'spekt] erwarten 6
expensive [ɪk'spensɪv] teuer 30
to explain [ɪk'spleɪn] erklären 26
to explode [ɪk'spləʊd] explodieren 61
to extend [ɪk'stend] erweitern 70
external hard drive [ɪkˌstɜ:nl 'hɑ:d‿ˌdraɪv] externe Festplatte 14
eye shadow ['aɪˌʃædəʊ] Lidschatten 38

F

fair trade [ˌfeə 'treɪd] fairer Handel 67
famous ['feɪməs] berühmt 45
far away [ˌfɑ:r‿ə'weɪ] weit weg 24
fashion shop ['fæʃn ˌʃɒp] Modegeschäft 8
fashionable ['fæʃnəbl] modisch 13
favour ['feɪvə] Gefallen 40
figure ['fɪgə] Zahl AP
to fire ['faɪə] entlassen 77
to fit [fɪt] passen 14
five-star hotel [ˌfaɪvstɑ: həʊ'tel] 5-Sterne Hotel 46
flammable ['flæməbl] entflammbar 54
flat rate ['flætreɪt] einheitlicher Kostensatz 48
floor [flɔ:] Stock(werk), Geschoss 37
flyer ['flaɪə] Werbeblatt 46
to follow ['fɒləʊ] folgen 22
foreground ['fɔ:graʊnd] Vordergrund 50
foreign branch [ˌfɒrən 'brɑ:ntʃ] ausländische Filiale 6
fragile ['frædʒaɪl] zerbrechlich 53
free of charge [ˌfri:‿əv 'tʃɑ:dʒ] kostenlos 72

fridge [frɪdʒ] Kühlschrank 26
from abroad [frəm ə'brɔ:d] aus dem Ausland 58
full-time *(adj)*, **full time** *(adv)* [ˌfʊltaɪm; ˌfʊl'taɪm] Vollzeit 78
fully qualified [ˌfʊlɪ 'kwɒlɪfaɪd] voll qualifiziert 78
furniture ['fɜ:nɪtʃə] Möbel 63
further ['fɜ:ðə] weiter 72

G

gap [gæp] Lücke 27
to get on sb's nerves (got, got) [ˌget ɒn ˌsʌmbədɪz 'nɜ:vz, gɒt, gɒt] jdm. auf die Nerven gehen 23
to get right [get 'raɪt] verstehen 58
to give up (gave, given) [gɪv‿'ʌp, geɪv, 'gɪvn] aufgeben 77
glove [glʌv] Handschuh 56
to go off (went, gone) [gəʊ‿'ɒf, went, gɒn] schlecht werden 54
to go well with [ˌgəʊ 'wel wɪθ] gut passen zu 14
to go wrong [ˌgəʊ 'rɒŋ] schief gehen 54
a good deal [ˌgʊd‿'di:l] ein gutes Angebot 32
goods [gʊdz] Waren 8
gradual ['grædʒʊəl] allmählich AP
to grant [grɑ:nt] gewähren 73
graph [grɑ:f] Diagramm AP
grid [grɪd] Gitter 75
ground floor [ˌgraʊnd 'flɔ:] Erdgeschoss 37
to grow (grew, grown) [grəʊ, gru:, grəʊn] wachsen 70
guarantee [ˌgærən'ti:] Garantie 23
to guess [ges] (er)raten 15

H

habit ['hæbɪt] Gewohnheit 21
to handle ['hændl] handhaben 53
hardly ['hɑ:dlɪ] kaum 16
to have contact with (had, had) [ˌhæv 'kɒntækt wɪð, hæd, hæd] Kontakt haben mit 9
to have exact change [hæv ɪgˌzækt‿'tʃeɪndʒ] es passend haben 30
to have sth left [hæv 'left] etw. übrig haben 30
healthy ['helθɪ] gesund 13
heat [hi:t] Hitze 54
helpline ['helplaɪn] telefonischer Beratungsdienst 62
history ['hɪstrɪ] Geschichte 34
to hit (hit, hit) [hɪt, hɪt, hɪt] schlagen AP
home-entertainment shop [ˌhəʊm entə'teɪnmənt ˌʃɒp] Geschäft für Unterhaltungselektronik 5
honey ['hʌnɪ] Honig 30
humidity [hju:'mɪdɪtɪ] Feuchtigkeit 54
to hunt [hʌnt] *hier:* suchen 77

I

to identify [aɪ'dentɪfaɪ] identifizieren 21
if you don't mind [ɪf jə ˌdəʊnt 'maɪnd] wenn es dir/Ihnen nichts ausmacht 33
to illustrate ['ɪləstreɪt] illustrieren 66
to improve [ɪm'pru:v] verbessern 74
in advance [ɪn‿əd'vɑ:ns] im Voraus 70
in cash [ɪn 'kæʃ] in bar 74
in a hurry [ˌɪn‿ə 'hʌrɪ] in Eile 21
in instalments [ɪn ɪn'stɔ:lmənts] in Raten 74
in stock [ɪn 'stɒk] vorrätig 72
in the long run [ɪn ðə 'lɒŋ ˌrʌn] auf lange Sicht 61
in the meantime [ɪn ðə 'mi:ntaɪm] in der Zwischenzeit 65
to include [ɪn'klu:d] beinhalten 48
inconvenience [ˌɪnkən'vi:nɪəns] Unannehmlichkeit 58
to increase ['ɪnkri:s] zunehmen 47
to inform [ɪn'fɔ:m] informieren 57
information desk [ˌɪnfə'meɪʃn ˌdesk] Informationsschalter 39
to interrupt [ˌɪntə'rʌpt] unterbrechen 69
to introduce [ˌɪntrə'dju:s] einführen 46
to introduce sb to sb [ˌɪntrə'dju:s] jdn. jdm. vorstellen 7
to invent [ɪn'vent] erfinden 45
to invite [ɪn'vaɪt] einladen 46
invoice ['ɪnvɔɪs] Rechnung 74
to iron [aɪən] bügeln 54
item ['aɪtəm] Artikel 62

J

jewellery ['dʒu:əlrɪ] Schmuck 10
job centre ['dʒɒb ˌsentə] Arbeitsamt 77
job duty ['dʒɒb ˌdju:tɪ] Arbeitsaufgabe 8
job interview ['dʒɒb ˌɪntəvju:] Bewerbungsgespräch 79
journey ['dʒɜ:nɪ] Reise 82

K

to keep (kept, kept) [ki:p, kept, kept] (sich) halten (an) 55
to keep one's eyes open [ˌki:p wʌnz 'aɪz ˌəʊpn] die Augen offen halten 32
to keep sb satisfied [ki:pˌsʌmbədɪ 'sætɪsfaɪd] jdn. zufrieden stellen 22

key word ['ki: ˌwɜ:d] Stichwort 34
kids' zone ['kɪdzˬzəʊn] Kinderbereich 23
kind [kaɪnd] freundlich 23

L

label ['leɪbl] Etikett 22
launch [lɔ:ntʃ] Start 46
leaflet ['li:flɪt] Prospekt 32
leather goods ['leðə ˌgʊdz] Lederwaren 33
to leave (left, left) [li:v, left, left] (ver)lassen 21
leisure time [ˌleʒətaɪm] Freizeit 66
letter of application [ˌletərˬəvˬæplɪ'keɪʃn] Bewerbungsschreiben 77
to lie [laɪ] lügen 82
lift [lɪft] Aufzug 39
lipstick ['lɪpstɪk] Lippenstift 38
a loaf of [ə 'ləʊfˬəv] ein Laib 30
to lock [lɒk] abschließen 59
to look forward to [lʊk 'fɔ:wəd tu:] sich freuen auf 37
to lose (lost, lost) [lu:z, lɒst, lɒst] verlieren 58
lunch break ['lʌntʃ ˌbreɪk] Mittagspause 38

M

mark [mɑ:k] Note 78
married ['mærɪd] verheiratet 25
to match [mætʃ] zuordnen 8
meaning ['mi:nɪŋ] Bedeutung 10
to meet (met, met) [mi:t, met, met] (sich) treffen 6
to meet sb's needs [mi:t ˌsʌmbədɪz 'ni:dz] die Bedürfnisse von jdm. befriedigen 62
to miss [mɪs] vermissen 18
mobile phone [ˌməʊbaɪl 'fəʊn] Handy 47
mood [mu:d] Stimmung 9
mother tongue [ˌmʌðə 'tʌŋ] Muttersprache 80
to move [mu:v] bewegen 43

N

nail polish remover ['neɪl ˌpɒlɪʃ rɪˌmu:və] Nagellackentferner 38
nail scissors ['neɪl ˌsɪzəz] Nagelschere 38
news [nju:z] Nachricht(en) 37
next to ['nekst tʊ] neben 5

O

obviously ['ɒbvɪəslɪ] offensichtlich 22
odd one out [ˌɒd wʌnˬ'aʊt] nicht dazugehören 11
to offer ['ɒfə] (an)bieten 16
old-fashioned [ˌəʊld'fæʃnd] altmodisch 13
on receipt [ɒn rɪ'si:t] bei Erhalt 74
on time [ɒn 'taɪm] pünktlich 63
once [wʌns] einmal 9
opposite ['ɒpəzɪt] gegenüber 38
order ['ɔ:də] Bestellung 72
originally [ə'rɪdʒɪnəlɪ] ursprünglich 33
out of order [ˌaʊtˬəv 'ɔ:də] außer Betrieb 39
overpriced [ˌəʊvə'praɪst] überteuert 32
owner ['əʊnə] Besitzer/in 24

P

packaging ['pækɪdʒɪŋ] Verpackung 21
a packet of [ə 'pækɪtˬəv] eine Packung 30
particularly [pə'tɪkjʊləlɪ] besonders 16
partly ['pa:tlɪ] teilweise 16
part-time *(adj)*, **part time** *(adv)* [ˌpɑ:tˬtaɪm; ˌpɑ:tˬ'taɪm] Teilzeit 78
to pass [pɑ:s] bestehen 10
past [pɑ:st] vorbei 63
percentage [pə'sentɪdʒ] Prozentsatz 66
period of time [ˌpɪərɪədˬəv 'taɪm] Zeitraum 48
personnel manager [ˌpɜ:sən'el ˌmænɪdʒə] Personalchef 79
pet [pet] Haustier 55
pharmacist ['fɑ:məsɪst] Apotheker 45
phrase [freɪz] Redewendung 6
to pick up [pɪk 'ʌp] abholen 6
picture frame ['pɪktʃə ˌfreɪm] Bilderrahmen 23
pineapple ['paɪnæpl] Ananas 30
to place [pleɪs] *hier:* erteilen 73
place of work [ˌpleɪsˬəv 'wɜ:k] Arbeitsplatz 5
Pleased to meet you. [ˌpli:zdˬtə 'mi:tˬju:] Schön Sie/dich/euch kennen zu lernen. 6
polite [pə'laɪt] höflich 55
portable ['pɔ:təbl] tragbar 13
to practise ['præktɪs] üben 16
to praise [preɪz] loben 57
press release ['pres rɪˌli:s] Pressemitteilung 62
previous ['pri:vɪəs] vorherig AP
price tag ['praɪs ˌtæg] Preisschild 16
primary school ['praɪmərɪ ˌsku:l] Grundschule 80
prize [praɪz] Preis(gewinn) 46
production [prə'dʌkʃn] Herstellung 47
promise ['prɒmɪs] Versprechen 40
to protect [prə'tekt] schützen 54
public relations [ˌpʌblɪk rɪ'leɪʃnz] Öffentlichkeitsarbeit 45
pump [pʌmp] Pumpe 23
purchase ['pɜ:tʃəs] Einkauf 55

Q

quantity ['kwɒntətɪ] Menge 30

R

range of products [ˌreɪndʒ‿əv 'prɒdʌkts] Produktpalette 70
reason ['ri:zn] Grund 5
recall ['ri:kɔ:l] Rückrufaktion 61
receipt [rɪ'si:t] Quittung 17
receipt of order [rɪˌsi:t‿əv 'ɔ:də] Auftragseingang 72
to receive [rɪ'si:v] empfangen 27
to recommend [ˌrekə'mend] empfehlen 57
reduction [rɪ'dʌkʃn] Ermäßigung 33
reference line ['refrəns ˌlaɪn] Bezugszeichenzeile 65
refund ['ri:fʌnd] (Rück)Erstattung 62
regulation [ˌregjə'leɪʃn] Vorschrift 55
to rely on [rɪ'laɪ‿ɒn] sich verlassen auf 64
to remember [rɪ'membə] sich erinnern (an) 42
to remind [rɪ'maɪnd] erinnern 73
to repair [rɪ'peə] reparieren 39
repayment [rɪ'peɪmənt] Rückzahlung 34
to repeat [rɪ'pi:t] wiederholen 58
replacement [rɪ'pleɪsmənt] Ersatz 56
reply [rɪ'plaɪ] Antwort 70
reputation [ˌrepjʊ'teɪʃn] Ruf, Ansehen 10
to request [rɪ'kwest] bitten 70
to resist [rɪ'zɪst] widerstehen 46
result [rɪ'zʌlt] Ergebnis 24
retail chain ['ri:teɪl ˌtʃeɪn] Einzelhandelskette 6
return [rɪ'tɜ:n] Rückgabe 72
to rise (rose, risen) [raɪz, rəʊz, 'rɪzn] steigen AP
a roll of [ə 'rəʊl‿əv] eine Rolle 30
to ruin ['ru:ɪn] ruinieren 56
rule [ru:l] Regel 54

S

sales promotion [ˌseɪlzprə'məʊʃn] Verkaufsförderung 47
salutation [ˌsæljʊ'teɪʃn] Anrede 65
sample ['sɑ:mpl] Muster 53
sausage ['sɒsɪdʒ] Würstchen 17
to save [seɪv] sparen 33
sceptic ['skeptɪk] skeptisch, kritisch 21
scratch [skrætʃ] Kratzer 57
screen [ˌskri:n] Bildschirm 26
search engine ['sɜ:tʃ ˌendʒɪn] Suchmaschine 34
secondary school ['sekəndrɪ ˌsku:l] weiterführende Schule 80
to see a point (saw, seen) [ˌsi:‿ə 'pɔɪnt, sɔ:, si:n] einen Standpunkt verstehen 56
to serve [sɜ:v] bedienen 8
service ['sɜ:vɪs] Dienstleistung 13
settlement ['setlmənt] Bezahlung 72
to share [ʃeə] teilen 63
sharp [ʃɑ:p] scharf AP
shelf [ʃelf] Regal 6
shop assistant ['ʃɒp‿əˌsɪstnt] Verkäufer/in 8
shop fittings ['ʃɒp ˌfɪtɪŋz] Ladenausstattung 24
showroom ['ʃəʊru:m] Ausstellungsraum 26
signature ['sɪgnətʃə] Unterschrift 65
size [saɪz] Größe 23
to smell [smel] riechen 53
smoking area ['sməʊkɪŋ ˌeərɪə] Raucherzone 55
soldier ['səʊldʒə] Soldat/in 48
to solve [sɒlv] lösen 56
to sort [sɔ:t] sortieren 8
special offer [ˌspeʃl‿'ɒfə] Sonderangebot 14
specialist shop ['speʃəlɪst ˌʃɒp] Fachgeschäft 24
to spend (spent, spent) [spend, spent, spent] ausgeben 62
state [steɪt] Staat 45
statement ['steɪtmənt] Aussage 7
to station ['steɪʃn] stationieren 48
to stay [steɪ] bleiben 39
storage capacity ['stɔ:rɪdʒ kəˌpæsɪtɪ] Speicherkapazität 16
to store [stɔ:] (ab)speichern 15
straight on [streɪt 'ɒn] geradeaus 39
to study ['stʌdɪ] studieren, sorgfältig lesen 22
stylish ['staɪlɪʃ] elegant 13
subject ['sʌbdʒekt] Fach 81
subject line ['sʌbdʒekt ˌlaɪn] Betreffzeile 65
subscription [səb'skrɪpʃn] Abonnement 74
successfully [sək'sesfəlɪ] erfolgreich 17
suggestion [sə'dʒestʃn] Vorschlag 56
to suit [su:t] (jdm.) stehen 14
suitcase ['su:tkeɪs] Koffer 64
to sum up [sʌm 'ʌp] zusammenfassen 6
supplier [sə'plaɪə] Lieferant 69
survey ['sɜ:veɪ] Umfrage, Befragung 25

T

table ['teɪbl] Tabelle 8
to tag [tæg] auszeichnen 8
to take care of (took, taken) [ˌteɪk‿'keər‿əv, tʊk, 'teɪkn] aufpassen auf 23
to take notes [teɪk 'nəʊts] Notizen machen 10

to take one's time [ˌteɪk wʌnz ˈtaɪm] sich Zeit nehmen 21
to take part [ˌteɪk ˈpɑːt] teilnehmen 25
target group [ˈtɑːɡɪt ˌɡruːp] Zielgruppe 50
task [tɑːsk] Aufgabe 8
taste [teɪst] Geschmack 33
temporary job [ˌtemprərɪ ˈdʒɒb] befristete Stelle 78
terms of delivery and payment [ˌtɜːmz‿əv dɪˌlɪvərɪ‿ən ˈpeɪmənt] Lieferungs- und Zahlungsbedingungen 70
text messaging [ˈtekst ˌmesɪdʒɪŋ] Textmitteilung 47
top floor [ˌtɒp ˈflɔː] Obergeschoss 37
to touch [tʌtʃ] anfassen 53
toy [tɔɪ] Spielzeug 39
trade discount [ˌtreɪd‿ˈdɪskaʊnt] Handelsnachlass 70
trainee [ˌtreɪˈniː] Auszubildende/r 6
traineeship [ˌtreɪˈniːʃɪp] Ausbildung 6
training to become [bɪ ˌtreɪnɪŋ tʊ bɪˈkʌm] in der Ausbildung sein zum/zur 9
travel guide [ˈtrævl ˌɡaɪd] Reiseführer 54
trolley [ˈtrɒlɪ] Einkaufswagen 22
trust [ˈtrʌst ɪn] Vertauen 61
truth [ˈtruːθ] Wahrheit 82
to try (on) [traɪ] (an)probieren 10
twice as much as [ˌtwaɪs‿əz ˈmʌtʃ‿əz] zweimal so viel wie 30

U

to underline [ˌʌndəˈlaɪn] unterstreichen 6
unfortunately [ʌnˈfɔːtʃnətlɪ] leider 55
to unpack [ʌnˈpæk] auspacken 8
to unsettle [ʌnˈsetl] beunruhigen 61
unsure [ʌnˈʃɔː] unsicher 49
upright [ˈʌpraɪt] aufrecht 82
upset [ʌpˈset] aufgebracht 56

V

vocational school [vəʊˈkeɪʃnl ˌskuːl] Berufsschule 9
voucher [ˈvaʊtʃə] Gutschein 56

W

wallet [ˈwɒlɪt] Geldbeutel 32
to weigh [weɪ] wiegen 47
well-designed [ˌwel dɪˈzaɪnd] gut gestaltet 13
with reference to [wɪð ˈrefrəns tuː] mit Bezug auf 70
to withdraw (withdrew, withdrawn) [wɪðˈdrɔː, wɪðˈdruː, wɪðˈdrɔːn] abheben 29
work experience [ˈwɜːk ɪkˌspɪərɪəns] Berufserfahrung 80
wristwatch [ˈrɪstwɒtʃ] Armbanduhr 69

Y

You're welcome. [ˌjɔː ˈwelkəm] Bitte schön, gern geschehen. 16

Abbildungsnachweis

COVER MEV Verlag GmbH, Augsburg; **COVER** Avenue Images; **COVER** (Marcus Schmigelski); **COVER** f1 online digitale Bildagentur (RFJohnér), Frankfurt; **2** Fotolia LLC (Franz Pfluegl), New York; **2** JupiterImages photos.com (photos.com), Tucson, AZ; **2** Bananastock RF, Watlington/Oxon; **2** iStockphoto (Manuela Krause), Calgary, Alberta; **2** shutterstock (Stavchansky Yakov), New York, NY; **2** MEV Verlag GmbH, Augsburg; **3** Dreamstime LLC (Scott Griessel), Brentwood, TN; **3** JupiterImages photos.com, Tucson, AZ; **3** Fotosearch Stock Photography (Banana Stock), Waukesha, WI; **3** iStockphoto (Sean Locke), Calgary, Alberta; **5** Dreamstime LLC (Pavel Losevsky), Brentwood, TN; **5** iStockphoto (Brasil2), Calgary, Alberta; **5** shutterstock (Vling), New York, NY; **5** Fotolia LLC (Franz Pfluegl), New York; **6** Fotolia LLC (Franz Pfluegl), New York; **8** shutterstock (Factoria singular fotografia), New York, NY; **8** shutterstock (iofoto), New York, NY; **8** Fotolia LLC (Fotolia XI), New York; **8** JupiterImages photos.com, Tucson, AZ; **9** JupiterImages photos.com, Tucson, AZ; **10** shutterstock (Andreas Gradin), New York, NY; **10** shutterstock (Clara Natoli), New York, NY; **10** shutterstock (milinz), New York, NY; **10** iStockphoto (pederk), Calgary, Alberta; **13** iStockphoto (Alexandra Draghici), Calgary, Alberta; **13** iStockphoto (Dan Herrick), Calgary, Alberta; **13** iStockphoto (RF/Achim Prill), Calgary, Alberta; **13** shutterstock (coka), New York, NY; **14** Fotolia LLC (Franz Pfluegl), New York; **15** Bananastock RF, Watlington/Oxon; **15** iStockphoto/Anton Ovcharenko; **15** iStockphoto (Josef Philipp), Calgary, Alberta; **15** shutterstock (Losevsky Pavel), New York, NY; **16** shutterstock (Losevsky Pavel), New York, NY; **17** Imago Stock & People, Berlin; **17** OBI, Wermelskirchen; **17** Burger King GmbH, München; **19** shutterstock (konstantynov), New York, NY; **21** MEV Verlag GmbH, Augsburg; **21** Ullstein Bild GmbH (Grabowsky), Berlin; **21** iStockphoto (ALEAIMAGE), Calgary, Alberta; **21** shutterstock (Diego Cervo), New York, NY; **22** JupiterImages photos.com, Tucson, AZ; **23** iStockphoto (Don Bayley), Calgary, Alberta; **23** iStockphoto (Ekaterina Monakhova), Calgary, Alberta; **23** Fotosearch Stock Photography (Digital Vision), Waukesha, WI; **24** MEV Verlag GmbH, Augsburg; **24** Klett-Archiv (Patricia Neumann), Stuttgart; **24** shutterstock (olly), New York, NY; **25** Avenue Images GmbH (Imgram Publishing), Hamburg; **25** JupiterImages photos.com, Tucson, AZ; **26** shutterstock (iDesign), New York, NY; **27** Klett-Archiv (Naudin), Stuttgart; **29** Alamy Images RM (vario images), Abingdon, Oxon; **29** iStockphoto (Winston Davidian), Calgary, Alberta; **29** iStockphoto (Manuela Krause), Calgary, Alberta; **29** iStockphoto (binagel), Calgary, Alberta; **29** www.cartoonstock.com (Stan Eales), Bath; **30** iStockphoto (Sean Locke), Calgary, Alberta; **31** shutterstock (Ocean Image Photography), New York, NY; **31** shutterstock (Neptune), New York, NY; **31** iStockphoto (Kevin Thomas), Calgary, Alberta; **31** iStockphoto (Günay Mutlu), Calgary, Alberta; **32** iStockphoto (DSGpro), Calgary, Alberta; **32** iStockphoto (Linda Steward), Calgary, Alberta; **32** iStockphoto (Eric Gevaert), Calgary, Alberta; **32** shutterstock (Timothy Geiss), New York, NY; **33** Dreamstime LLC (Alexandr Dvorak), Brentwood, TN; **34** Avenue Images GmbH (Comstock), Hamburg; **34** Fotosearch Stock Photography, Waukesha, WI; **35** shutterstock (androfroll), New York, NY; **35** Avenue Images GmbH (IT Stock Free), Hamburg; **35** iStockphoto (Linda Steward), Calgary, Alberta; **35** shutterstock (Joel Kempson), New York, NY; **37** shutterstock (Stavchansky Yakov), New York, NY; **37** Dreamstime LLC (Pavel Losevsky), Brentwood, TN; **37** shutterstock (Jonathan Feinstein), New York, NY; **37** shutterstock (Ragne Kabanova), New York, NY; **38** JupiterImages photos.com, Tucson, AZ; **39** shutterstock (Diego Cervo), New York, NY; **40** JupiterImages photos.com, Tucson, AZ; **41** shutterstock (Letova), New York, NY; **41** iStockphoto (Mike Panic), Calgary, Alberta; **41** shutterstock (Nikolay Postnikov), New York, NY; **42** Dream Maker Software (RF), Colorado; **43** shutterstock (Diana Nickels), New York, NY; **45** Coca-Cola GmbH, Essen; **45** Interfoto, München; **45** JupiterImages photos.com (photos.com), Tucson, AZ; **46** MEV Verlag GmbH, Augsburg; **46** shutterstock (Raisa Kanareva), New York, NY; **47** JupiterImages photos.com, Tucson, AZ; **49** Vodafone D2 GmbH, Düsseldorf; **50** iStockphoto (René Mansi), Calgary, Alberta; **51** POWER HORSE Energy Drinks GmbH, Linz; **53** Dell GmbH, Frankfurt; **53** Ingram Publishing, Tattenhall Chester; **53** shutterstock (Losevsky Pavel), New York, NY; **53** iStockphoto (Lai Leng Yiap), Calgary, Alberta; **53** Roberto Degli Innocenti, Pistoia; **54** shutterstock (Christoph Weihs), New York, NY; **54** Klett-Archiv, Stuttgart; **54** shutterstock (Albo003), New York, NY; **56** shutterstock (Sergey Rusakov), New York, NY; **61** shutterstock (Hadi Djunaedi), New York, NY; **61** shutterstock (Rafa Irusta), New York, NY; **61** iStockphoto (aida ricciardiello caballero), Calgary, Alberta; **61** shutterstock (Dario Sabljak), New York, NY; **62** iStockphoto (pkruger), Calgary, Alberta; **63** shutterstock (Monkey Business Images), New York, NY; **64** www.cartoonstock.com (Morris, John), Bath; **69** shutterstock (vgstudio), New York, NY; **69** shutterstock (Dean Mitchell), New York, NY; **69** Avenue Images GmbH (Comstock), Hamburg; **69** Avenue Images GmbH (Image Source), Hamburg; **69** shutterstock (Yuri Arcurs), New York, NY; **72** iStockphoto (volk65), Calgary, Alberta; **72** MEV Verlag GmbH (MEV-Verlag GmbH, Augsburg), Augsburg; **72** Thamphald, Sven; **75** shutterstock (MaGutosh), New York, NY; **77** Fotosearch Stock Photography (PhotoDisc), Waukesha, WI; **77** shutterstock (Juan David Ferrando Subero), New York, NY; **77** shutterstock (Dmitriy Shironosov), New York, NY; **77** shutterstock (Le Loft 1911), New York, NY; **77** JupiterImages photos.com, Tucson, AZ; **78** Avenue Images GmbH (StockDisc), Hamburg; **80** Klett-Archiv (A. Raftaki), Stuttgart; **81** Klett-Archiv (A. Raftaki), Stuttgart; **83** Corel Corporation Deutschland, Unterschleissheim; **83** iStockphoto (RF/Adam Booth), Calgary, Alberta; **83** iStockphoto (Lance Bellers), Calgary, Alberta; **83** Fotolia LLC (Jerome Dancette), New York; **Activity Page** shutterstock (Vishal Shah), New York, NY; **Activity Page** Avenue Images GmbH (StockDisc), Hamburg; **KMK** Avenue Images GmbH (Image Source), Hamburg

Nicht in allen Fällen war es uns möglich, den Rechteinhaber der Abbildungen ausfindig zu machen. Berechtigte Ansprüche werden selbstverständlich im Rahmen der üblichen Vereinbarungen abgegolten.